To Cousin Susan —
Happy reading —
Joan

Stories

And

Selected

Essays

By

Joan O. King

Illustrated by the Author

Acknowledgments

A general thanks to family and friends who have seen me through so many ups and downs in my life. Without each and every one of you I would be, in the words of my late husband, "like a lost ball in the high weeds". Lewis, my love, I miss you more than you can imagine.

Special thanks to the Thorbeckes, Lea and Herman, who helped me publish Stories and Selected Essays and to my dear friend Glenn Carroll who edited the book.

In addition I want to thank the Clarkesville Writers Society. For many years its members have met at our local library to encourage and nurture one another. It is through them I discovered the joy of writing. Folks, you know who you are. I am forever in your debt.

I also want to thank the Gainesville Times who, for over fifteen years, employed me as a guest columnist. The discipline of producing 650 words on deadline taught me to take my writing seriously, and the insight gained from reader's response enriched my life.

And finally to an English teacher at Bucknell University who became exasperated with my inability to edit my own work and told me, "If you could just spell as well as you craft your sentences, there might be some hope for you as a writer." I don't remember your name, but your words have stuck with me for over sixty years.

Dedication
This book is dedicated to my late husband
Edward Lewis King
&
To my beloved grand daughter
Anna Scott King

CONTENTS

STORIES

The Garden

THE MYSTERY WOMAN

It seems appropriate to begin this book with a story about the Clarkesville Writing Group. When I read it to them, several of our long time members remembered the woman, but nobody knew what had happened to her. She just stopped showing up.

No one confirmed or denied the ending of the tale so I guess I can say it is true, but then we all have a vivid imagination. I leave it to the reader to decide.

The Clarkesville Writing Group meets in the Community Room of the local library every Friday at ten. We're a mixed group. All serious writers, some of us have published poems or articles in writing magazines, some have self-published a novel or two. One is even a long-time guest columnist for a regional paper, but none of us could be considered "a professional writer."

Most of us are middle-aged or older, but younger people are more than welcome, and in the summer we sometimes swell our number with a college student or two. It's a diverse group with diverse interests. We write memoirs, adventure stories, romance, even science fiction. The only rule is: no religion, no politics.

Avoiding these divisive issues, the group has remained harmonious over an extended period of time. We appreciate and even nurture one another. Over time, we have become familiar with each other's interests and idiosyncrasies. For instance, one member lost much of her childhood memory after brain surgery. Writing memoirs helps her regain her past.

Another member has traveled extensively and writes adventure stories. He writes in the first person and is a great storyteller, but it's best to take his tales with a grain of salt. A woman member writes openly about her family, stories that are revealing and poignant.

On one level we know a lot about one another; on another level, very little. The main thing we have in common is our love of writing and our active imaginations.

The Clarkesville Writing Group was formed more than a decade ago and has waxed and waned over the years. Leaders, whose primary job is to set reading and exercise times, have come and gone. It's a frustrating job. Keeping a bunch of creative people on task is like herding cats.

When someone new joins the group the leader introduces him or her and we go around the room. Each member says something about himself — what he or she has written and what he or she hopes to accomplish in the future. (Everyone, of course, has an unfinished novel on their computer or stored under the bed.)

One man, a rather unpretentious individual, about 5 foot eight, a hundred sixty pounds and balding, said he wanted to learn how to write a good story because he'd spent his life working for the CIA and needed to explain his many sudden absences and secretive behavior to his children. They never knew what Daddy did.

Of course, we all wanted to read that story but nobody asked. They knew the answer. "I could tell you, but then I'd have to kill you." The stories he did write during exercise time were usually about trains. The man loved trains.

For me these exercises were the high point of the meetings. They consisted of various "prompts." Sometimes it was a first line: "The cat stared... The door blew open... Whatever you do, don't..." Sometimes we went around the room and everyone said a word. The CIA guy always said "train." Then we'd all write like mad for twenty minutes or so.

Most of us were delighted to read what we'd written to the group, but no one was obliged to do so. No one thought it unusual. They just weren't ready. The woman I'm going to tell you about was one of those. She was a recent addition. Upon introducing herself she said she wrote mystery stories and was interested in the occult.

She participated in the exercises, writing furiously in a red leather notebook she carried in a large cloth bag slung over her shoulder, but when it came time to read she demurred saying that she didn't like what she wrote or simply wasn't ready to read it aloud. It was only after several months that we realized that she had *never* read anything, but then most of us were extroverts and didn't mind if someone chose not to read. It meant more time for those of us who did. The woman was simply quiet and a bit remote. If her dress and demeanor were a little odd... well, as I said, we all had our idiosyncrasies.

Our new addition was of indeterminate age and ethnicity. She had a long face and somewhat aristocratic features, but the most unusual thing about her countenance was that she could appear rather homely one minute and quite handsome the next. Her expression didn't change, but something did. Several of us had commented on it in private, but no one could quite figure it out. Was she ugly or strangely beautiful?

Around the first of the year someone suggested the Writing Group put together an anthology of our best stories. Our leader warned us of the difficulties, but I believe the rest of us had the same two things in mind: An opportunity to publish and a solution to next year's Christmas gifting.

The group formed a committee and began to consider submissions. Again, the rules were few: three thousand words or less, three submissions allowed, and the author had to have attended the Group on a regular basis for at least two months.

On any given Friday we might have as few as four or five people or as many as twelve or more. Upon arriving we all pitch in to set up the folding tables stored in a small kitchen area and pull out the padded chairs stacked around the walls. The tables were sturdy affairs about six feet long and two feet wide. Two of them placed parallel to one another would accommodate up to six people.

Three placed in a triangle would seat two on each side and as many as three more in the obtuse angles where the tables met. While this arrangement seated nine people, it was far from ideal since those seated in the angles were forced to turn their back on another member if they needed a solid surface upon which to write.

When more than eight were present, we set up four tables touching at their inner corners and forming an empty square in the middle. However, when our numbers increased as they had recently we added a fifth table, which formed a pentagon.

One particularly oppressive summer's day in June members drifted in slowly and began setting up the tables. When I arrived there were four tables set in a large square. As more people wandered in, more chairs were called for. The number grew to twelve, but nobody had the energy to add a fifth table. Then about quarter after ten a thirteenth person arrived. It was our mystery woman.

She stood there dressed in a gauzy black caftan that reached to the floor, a rather unusual choice of dress for such a hot day. The only color visible was a startling slash of red lipstick. This alone did not attract any particular attention. We were an accepting bunch and rather admired the woman's ability to carry off some rather bizarre dress wear. However, we were put off by her late arrival because it meant we could no longer manage without adding a fifth table. Everybody would have to move.

The fifth table was set up and jockeyed into place. The woman in black seemed overly interested in placing the tables so that their corners just touched and the new configuration was situated precisely in the middle of the room. The woman was obviously compulsive as well as strange. People rearranged themselves, and the woman took a seat near one of the corners.

The room became suddenly and strangely silent. Our loyal leader stood and announced that this was the last day for submissions to the anthology. Did anyone have anything?

"I do," and the woman stood. As we all watched, she moved one of the tables a few inches, slipped into the middle of the pentagon, and closed the opening behind her. We all stared, and she began:

"When I joined your group..." she was speaking slowly... "I said I wrote mystery stories." Now she was moving to face each one of us in turn. "I don't. I *create* mystery stories."

She continued her slow turn until she had looked directly into every pair of eyes in the room. "This is my submission." Whereupon she opened the cloth bag she carried over her shoulder and produced a small brown-paper grocery bag.

Opening it carefully she again turned so each of us could see the bag was empty. Mesmerized by her voice, and her slow deliberate movement and flowing garb, no one said anything. "Now!" Her tone was commanding. "Keep your eyes on the bag."

With that, she set the bag in the center of the room, quickly opened a space at the corner of two of the tables, exited the pentagon, readjusted the tables, and left the room.

I couldn't move. Neither could anyone else, but the bag could... and it did. It made a little crackling sound as if straightening out one of its folds. Just a small scratchy sound, nothing more. We all stared.

Then, just as someone was about to break the spell, the bag began to float. It couldn't have been but a fraction of an inch, but we could all see a space growing under the bag. It was beginning to levitate. Slowly, very slowly, the bag rose, first a foot or so, then to the level of the tables, and then... again, very slowly... to the ceiling where it rested.

No one remembers what happened after that. When someone came to the door to see if we were through with the room, the clock read 12:15. Twelve stunned people sat

around the tables. A crumpled paper bag lay on the floor.
We never saw the woman again.

Untitled

HALLOWEEN

Any holiday is an excuse for a party and a prompt for us writers. This story was started the week of Halloween and completed at home in the following days.

"I won't do it Nancy. I won't."

Nancy had never heard Caroline say anything so emphatic in all the years she'd known her. It was totally out of character.

Nancy met Caroline at the school bus stop one September morning when both their daughters were starting first grade. The two little girls were wide-eyed and apprehensive as their mothers loaded them into the big yellow school bus. Caroline, however, was closer to tears than her curly-headed little Hannah. Nancy put her hand on the young woman's arm, assured her everything would be O.K., and took her home for coffee and some comforting words.

Caroline had been new in the neighborhood, and Hannah was her only child. Caroline needed a friend. Nancy's daughter Betsy, a tough little brunette, was the youngest of three. The others were in high school, and Nancy was facing an empty nest. She needed a project.

The two women took to each other immediately. They'd been best friends now for five years, more like sisters actually, the older woman outgoing and outspoken, the younger quiet, obliging, and eager to please. It was rare that

10

Caroline questioned Nancy's suggestions. This wasn't questioning. It was out and out revolt. Caroline wanted no part in a neighborhood Haunted House.

"For Heaven sake, Caroline, why not? It's better for children to be in the Rogers' back yard where their parents can watch over them than wandering around from house to house taking candy from God Knows Who."

The Rogers lived at the end of a cul-de-sac and had an abandoned cabin in the woods behind their house. Nancy had decided it would be the perfect spot for a Haunted House. Several of the neighborhood parents agreed and offered to pitch in. Now Caroline, her best friend, her protégé, had dug in her heels and closed her ears to reason.

"What in the world is the matter with you, Caroline? Kids love a Haunted House, and it would be fun for all of us. I've got all sorts of good ideas for decorations. Look at this magazine. Goblin costumes. Smoking cauldrons. A Dracula mask. We'll all have a ball."

"Sure," replied Caroline. "Let's just scare the bejesus out of the kids."

"Caroline, they know it's fake, and child psychologists say Halloween is actually good for kids. It's a way to face their fears. They get a little bit scared, but it's O.K. They know their parents are close by and there to protect them."

"Nancy, I wasn't allowed to take part in Halloween when I was growing up. My mother said it was un-Christian."

Ghouls

12

"But, Caroline, you've put all that behind you. You told me you finally stood up to your mother, and you're not religious. You don't believe it's evil to let kids dress up like ghosts or goblins. Remember the great witch costumes we made for our girls when they were in that school play last year?"

"I know, Nancy. I don't want anything to do with a haunted house. That's all," and Caroline's face got that blank look she always had when an issue was closed. Nancy knew when she was beaten and changed the subject.

"Have you tried that recipe for pork tenderloin, the one the paper ran in the food section the other day?" Nancy said. But Caroline's expression didn't change. Her mind was elsewhere. She was back in her parents' house almost 20 years ago. It was mid-October, and she had just gotten home from school.

"Mom, it's less than two weeks till Halloween. I've got to have a costume for the school party."

"I know dear. I'm making it for you," Caroline's mother said stiffly. She was a good seamstress, but that wasn't the point.

"Mom, I'm not going to school as Little Bo Peep. I'm not," Caroline whined but she knew it was hopeless. Her mother always won. She had already embarrassed Caroline by going to the school board with her complain about Halloween. She told them that dedicating a day to devils, witches, and the undead was a form of Satanism, and when she enlisted some people from a nearby fundamentalist church to back her up, the school board caved.

The school compromised a bit by allowing pumpkins and black and orange decorations in the classrooms and by proceeding with the traditional Halloween costume party, but they forbade anything that might offend the more sensitive parents. In other words, devils, ghosts, zombies, and Dracula, were out. Disney and some of the more benign fairy tale characters were in. Of course, the word got back to the neighborhood children that Caroline's mother was the reason they couldn't dress up in all those ghoulish costumes they loved. Caroline was mortified.

Caroline hadn't exactly told Nancy the truth when she said her mother was a religious fanatic. Actually, the family was Presbyterian, and a fairly liberal branch of the church at that.

But Mrs. Cunningham *was* a fanatic, the kind of person who was absolutely sure about everything. Toothpaste must be white paste. Red gels would make them sick. No colored toilet paper either. It gave people hemorrhoids. She even refused to use a dishwasher because it shortened the life of her dishes.

This meant that Caroline and her older brothers had to wash the dishes by hand, which did shorten the life of any number of glasses and other crockery when soapy items slipped out of careless fingers. Caroline had dropped a couple herself, and not entirely by accident.

In short, Caroline's mother was an opinionated, domineering, busybody who proved to be a source of constant embarrassment to Caroline and her two older brothers. Her brothers were twins: Nicholas and Richard--- Nick and Rick to their friends. The boys managed to stay out their mother's way as much as possible, but Caroline couldn't escape as easily and had learned to take the course of least resistance. She avoided conflict by agreeing with whatever her mother wanted and was much admired by her mother's friends for being a docile and obliging daughter.

However, this Halloween was going to be different. Caroline might have to be Little Bo Peep at the school party, but Nick and Rick were going to take her trick-or-treating instead of her father. "We can take care of her, Mom," said Nick. "Yah," echoed Rick. "We're both junior varsity. No one's going to mess with us. We'll look out for Caroline." Mrs. Cunningham looked doubtful.

"Mom," said Nick. "You know those fuzzy white bathrobes you made us for Christmas last year? We'll wear them, and you can make us hoods with little ears. You know, like sheep. We'll be Little Bo Peep's sheep."

That did it. Mrs. Cunningham couldn't resist showing off her talents with the sewing machine. Caroline should have been suspicious right then. It wasn't like her brothers to help her out, but they had been getting away with all kinds of things for years. They said they felt sorry and now they wanted to help her break out of the maternal cocoon.

Once the three of them were out of sight of the house, they said, she could ditch the Little Bo Peep costume and become anything she wanted. She could even come with them to a Haunted House the older kids in the neighborhood had designed. Caroline was delighted.

She wore the hated Bo Peep costume to the school party, but when she left the house with the twins that evening, Little Bo Peep's basket hid an old back dress Caroline had found in the attic, a roll of gauze from the family medicine chest, and a bottle of ketchup from the pantry.

15

The three Cunningham children stopped at the Roger's house next door for some candied apples, picked up some Snicker Bars at the McMann's house, and turned the corner. Caroline looked for some bushes to hide behind while she donned her improvised costume, but the twins stopped her.

"You've heard of wolves in sheep's clothing, haven't you Caroline?" said Nick.

"Just watch," said Rick, and both boys yanked off the furry hoods with the little sheep ears. From somewhere under the bathrobes they produced rubber wolf masks and pulled them over their heads.

"Little Bo Peep is going to the Haunted House..." Rick paused... "As our dinner. Ahh-wooooo," he howled convincingly.

"Come along like a good little girl," said Nick, as he slipped a rope around her waist and tied it in a knot. What was Caroline to think? These were her brothers. If she had any doubts about their intentions, she kept it to herself and did as she had for years—took the course of least resistance.

They walked a couple of blocks to Green Street passing other children who were out trick-or-treating. If anyone thought it was odd for two boys with wolf masks to be leading Little Bo Peep on a rope... well, the girl didn't seem to be protesting, and after all, it was Halloween.

It was easy to pick out the Haunted House, an old Victorian home in the middle of the block lit by candles in the windows and some sort of pulsing purple light coming from the open door. Caroline knew it belonged to the

Richardsons who had several teenaged children popular with the in-crowd. Caroline began to get excited. This might turn out to be great. It certainly was something none of the other sixth graders would get to do.

They climbed the stairs to the porch where an assortment of goblins, ghouls, and zombies where hanging out. Apparently Nick and Rick were expected. When her brothers walked through the open door, the rest followed. They were greeted by a woman with long silver hair and a black and silver dress that came up high on the throat. She wore a mask, but Caroline was pretty sure it was Veronica, Rick's current girlfriend. The figure turned around, and Caroline saw that the dress was cut very low in the back. Every inch of exposed flesh was covered with tattoos. Caroline was impressed. She couldn't wait to tell the other girls in her class.

The deeper into the house they went, the darker it got. Strings or something hung from the ceiling, and they brushed against her face making her shiver. The floorboards creaked and she heard moaning sounds coming from someplace in the house. She wanted to hold Rick's hand, but there was nobody at the end of the rope. Rick was gone.

"Nick. Rick." she called softly. A deep voice in a commanding tone answered her. "Quiet, child." Suddenly her adventure wasn't turning out to be as much fun as she expected. The dark forms near her opened a side door and motioned her in. Something blew across her feet as she entered. Then all the lights went out.

Then the deep voice again from across the room: "What have you brought me?"

"A little girl, my Lord, a tender little morsel. Her name is Bo Peep."

"What shall we do with her?"

"Tear her in little pieces and eat her, My Lord."

"Are you sure? Perhaps we should keep her and make her one of us. Shall we put her to the test?"

"If that is your wish, My Lord. If she can pass the test we will not eat her."

"Child," the voice said ominously, "Do you want to join us?"

Caroline's throat was so dry she couldn't speak.

"Child," the voice boomed. "Are you ready to take the test? Yes or No."

Somehow Caroline managed a small trembling "yes."

"Bring her to me."

Someone lit a candle and Caroline was pushed forward toward a tall man wearing a cape and standing behind a table. On the table, only partially visible in the dim light, was a large bowl filled with long white twisting strands of something slimy.

"These are worms, Child, worms from the dead, dug from their graves this Halloween night. Thrust your hand in the bowl and draw out the key, the key that will make you one of us."

Caroline couldn't move. Someone grabbed her hand—it must have been Nick—and pulled her toward the table. Before she could resist, her hand was forced into the bowl of warm slippery worms. Her reaction was immediate. Not a scream, but a warm sensation between her legs. She could feel the urine soak through the pantaloons her mother had carefully sewn, run down her stockings, and puddle in her shoes.

Caroline didn't remember how she got out of the Haunted House. Her brothers must have realized what had happened and helped her escape in the darkness. Just the same, she was sure it would be all over school the next day. Caroline Cunningham had peed in her pants.

"It was spaghetti, Caroline. Friggin' spaghetti," Nick said as they walked home. "How could you be so dumb?"

Now, over twenty years later, Caroline still felt the sharp sting of humiliation. "No Nancy," she said "I won't do it. I want nothing to do with a haunted house!"

LIVING ALONE

*Living Alone **was written after my husband and I
moved to our home in the mountains. I was not actually
alone when a young man walked in through an open
door. He had a strange, confused look on his face that
unsettled me. Although Lewis was home, he was soaking
in our big claw-footed bathtub and in no position to
fend off an intruder.***

***My immediate response was to treat the young man
as a neighbor and offer him some of the cookies I was
baking. As it turned out the boy was visiting someone on
the other side of the mountain. He'd gone for a hike,
gotten lost just as the sun went down, and was thoroughly
shaken-up. He was no threat to anyone... but it could
have been different.***

Lorraine was dead set against her 70-year-old mother living
by herself in a cabin in the woods, but her mother was
nothing if not stubborn. Edna sat on the edge of her bed
listening to her daughter's voice over a cellphone.

"Mom, you don't even remember to lock your door."

"I don't forget," said Edna. She was becoming irritated. "I
don't like locks. I'm two miles back a dirt road in North
Georgia. Why should I lock the door?"

"Anybody could walk right in," replied Lorraine.

"Lorraine, I could lock the door; but if anybody wanted to
get in, all they have to do is break a window."

When Edna's husband died five years ago, the house in the mountains was still on the drawing boards. It was to have been their retirement home. The arguments started even before Harold was in the ground.

"Mom, you're not going to go ahead with the house and live up here all alone."

But Edna was adamant. "I certainly am," she said. "I'm looking forward to the solitude. I'm perfectly capable of taking care of myself."

They argued about everything, even the floor plan.

"Mom, you need to put the bathroom closer to your bedroom. You're not getting any younger, and you don't want to have to walk out into the hall when you get up at night."

"Lorraine. I don't *get* up at night. I sleep just fine, thank you. If I get to the point where I have a problem, I'll move back to town. It's too expensive to put in two bathrooms; and if you or anyone else stays in the loft, I don't want them stumbling into my bedroom if *they* have to get up at night."

Lorraine called every evening. Edna listened; but with increasing agitation. She shifted the little flip-phone to the other ear. Lorraine had insisted she buy it over a year ago.

"Mom", Lorraine had said, "if you must go walking in the woods, take your cellphone with you. If you get lost, you can call for help."

"Lorraine, I don't get lost. I'm exploring. I know where I am. There's only so much land on this mountain and then

21

you come to a road. When I come to a road, I know where I am."

In fact, Edna *had* gotten lost a couple of times wandering on the cliffs above the house. Once it was dark before she found her way back to the lane that led to her driveway. She'd been excited by the experience, pleased that she had not panicked and had carefully worked her way down the mountain and to the road; but she made the mistake of talking about her adventure, and the story got back to Lorraine who promptly went ballistic.

"You must promise, Mom. You must promise. Give me your word you'll always carry your cellphone with you when you go out."

The phone had become a weapon in Lorraine's battle to undermine her mother's self-confidence and dampen Edna's determination to live alone. Each time Lorraine came to visit, she asked where it was. Usually Edna didn't know.

"Mom, how can you lose a telephone?"

"Lorraine, I didn't lose it! I just put it down somewhere. Phones are supposed to be in one place, connected to something, like the one in living room, not carried around." But Lorraine had won another round.

Then there were the car keys. Edna left them in the ignition. Lorraine acted as if her mother were senile.

"Mom, you simply can't leave your keys in the car."

"I don't leave them in the car when I am in the city, Lorraine. I always put them in my bag. Nobody's going to take my car up here."

This evening's conversation was like all the rest. The concern in Lorraine's voice was getting on her nerves. "Lorraine, I'm all right! I'll see you next week when I'm in town. Goodbye."

Edna closed the phone, and tossed it on the floor. Thoroughly irritated she stood up and kicked the offending object under the bed.

"And it can stay there," she thought. Edna refused to become paranoid. If she let Lorraine's negative thinking get to her, she wouldn't be able to continue living here. Once she began locking her door and worrying about her car, she would start hearing noises at night. She would begin checking under her bed and jumping at shadows. That would be the end of her independence.

The light was almost gone, and she could feel the temperature dropping. It was barely six o'clock, but she was chilled. She looked out the window at the distant mountains and thought about a hot bath.

Edna was always a bit restless this time of day. Too early for dinner. Too late for any more work. It was the cocktail hour, but with Harold gone and no one to talk to...well she refused to become one of those women who drink alone and gradually become dependent on alcohol for escape. She stretched and walked out into the hall.

The cabin only had the one real bedroom. The rest of the space was devoted to a large living area and a sleeping loft. A sliding glass door opened on to a patio with a spectacular view of the distant Appalachian Mountains.

Edna's mind was a blank as she stared out at the bare trees. She turned, walked into the bathroom, and began drawing water into the large claw foot tub. The tub had been Harold's pride and joy, the only thing he salvaged from his mother's farm, the only thing he insisted on when planning the cabin.

Now it was Edna's favorite retreat. She could submerge herself completely and withdraw from the world with only her mouth and her nose protruded from the steaming water. She undressed and settled into the tub. Thus indisposed she never heard the sliding glass door open and the young man step inside.

Quietly the intruder slid the door shut and surveyed the large open space before him. The sofa, the TV, an over-stuffed chair, a desk, the small dining table strewn with books and papers but no indication that anyone was going to eat there. The cabin's owner apparently ate at the kitchen counter where a single stool was drawn up to a place mat.

The man moved toward the steps leading to the sleeping loft. Cautiously he started up—one, two, three steps to the first landing. That was enough to see under the railing, across the carpeted floor and into the back corner of the loft. Twin beds, a dresser, and a couple of chairs. No sign that the space was being used.

He backed down and moved into the kitchen area. There was nothing on the stove, no signs of food preparation. He ran one hand over the counter top, over the microwave, and then up to the knives in a rack on the wall. The fingers hesitated and then moved on.

He turned toward the small hall, his hand trailing long the wall, past a small mirror and over the light switch. On one side of the hall were two sets of louvered doors. He opened one enough to see the washer-dryer combination inside. The next held clothes. This he checked with greater care looking for something he did not find.

Farther down the hall, the door to the bedroom stood open. The door next to him must be the bathroom. He placed his hand on the knob and could feel the warmth. He could smell the steam. Now he knew where the occupant was, but to be sure, he stepped into the bedroom his eyes slowly moving across the dresser, the bed, and the night stand. A man stared blankly back at him from a wooden frame. Another frame held a woman with two young children. Husband, daughter and grandchildren, the man thought, but from the looks of the closet, no one else lived here.

Now the man moved with more confidence. He stood for a moment, his hand on the bathroom door knob. Inside Edna was reading, one hand holding a paperback book above the water, the rest of her almost completely submerged. The water was beginning to cool, and Edna pulled her glasses off and tossed them and the book on to the bath mat. She slipped down deep into the tub just before the door opened. The man appeared to her through a haze of steam and water.

As her body convulsed, water sloshed over her face, and her breath caught deep in her throat. She didn't scream. Adrenaline rushed into her system, and she gripped the side of the tub, but otherwise she didn't move.

The man stared down at her expressionless. Edna's body was neither fat nor wasted with age, but the man noted the discolored spots on the back of her hand, the wispy gray hair clinging to her wet skull, and the lines of the mouth and neck. Whatever lay behind the stare, whatever emotion, her naked vulnerability aroused, it was not sex.

Adrenaline overcame paralysis, and Edna jerked to a sitting position. Pulling her knees up to her chest and using her arms to shield herself, she found her voice.

"My God, you scared me!"

The man didn't move. He continued to stare. The hot water, the fright, were making Edna's head swim. She said, "If you'd have told me you were coming, I'd have had your supper ready."

The man's face remained immobile. His eyes were impossible to read. Now Edna didn't wait for a response.

"Buddy, you're letting in the cold, and you're being rude. Get out, and let me get dressed. I'll fix you something to eat."

Something in the man changed. His hand withdrew a bit, hesitated and then dropped to his side. Still, he didn't move.

"Go on Buddy. Close that door, and let me get dressed. " Edna looked away and reached for a towel. When she looked back again the door was closed.

Edna stood up grasping the towel rod for support. Then she forced herself to move. One foot over the edge of the tub. Hold on to the towel rod. Don't slip. Foot on the mat. Now the other foot. Now dry off.

She had brought clean underwear from the dresser in the bedroom, but her outer garments were hanging in the closet. She fumbled in the dirty clothes hamper for something to put on. Edna could sense the man standing just outside the door, his hand poised on the door knob. Pulling a dirty sweat shirt over her wet hair, she retrieved her glasses from the mat and prepared to leave the moist womb of the bathroom. Her glasses had cooled, and they clouded over as she placed them on her warm, still damp face. Once again she saw the man through a haze of steam as she went through the door. He was paring an apple with one of the kitchen knives.

"I don't keep much meat here when I'm by myself, but I've got lots of eggs. How about I fix you some eggs? Put cheese on them. Fry up some potatoes and onions? You'd like that, Buddy?" She walked past him into the kitchen area.

"You got a beer?" the man said. His voice was thin and tense, younger than his face.

"Sure, Buddy. Sure. Least I think so. Let me look." She went to the refrigerator, knelt down and began rummaging in the back of the bottom shelf. He stood directly behind her. The skin on her back of her neck prickled. Behind the cokes and root beers she found a couple of Buds and handed one up to him without looking.

"Here you go," she said. The eggs and cheese were higher up. The lightheadedness returned as she started to stand, and she grabbed the edge of the refrigerator to steady herself.

Help me up, Buddy. Getting old. My legs won't hold me."

There was a moment's hesitation, and she felt his hand under her elbow. Still not looking at him, Edna took three eggs in one hand, the cheese in the other, and used her shoulder to push the refrigerator door closed. Then she turned and stepped toward the stove.

The man didn't move. The knife and the apple were in his right hand, the beer tucked under his forearm, his left hand hanging limply at his side.

"I'll fix us some coffee. Sit down. Sit down. Just push those papers aside, and sit down. Supper won't take long. I'll make some buttermilk biscuits. You like buttermilk biscuits, don't ya, Buddy?" He didn't answer.

Edna liked to cook. Chopping, stirring, fussing with food always relaxed her. Unlike many who live alone, she took pains with her meals. The kitchen was her domain. She began to fill the coffee percolator from the tap, her movements smooth and confident.

But she couldn't control her voice. She was babbling. "This is special coffee, Buddy. Costs more, but it's worth it. Comes from South America, or someplace like that. It will be ready in a minute. You just finish your beer, and I'll fix you a cup."

If he would just say something. She wanted to hear that voice again. She could tell nothing looking into the face. It was hard and completely devoid of expression. The voice, she thought. The voice will tell me what I need to know.

The coffee began to perk as she formed the biscuits and placed them in a small pan. The man moved away from the refrigerator but made no move to sit down. She could see his chest rise as he inhaled the strong coffee aroma.

28

Edna's mind was as blank as she could make it. She was relying on instinct and years of habit. She moved automatically, saying the first thing that came into her head, blotting out the past and future. But now she knew something more was required.

This was a test of her faith. She must not hope. She must not question. She must let go of everything and submerge herself in time as she had submerged herself in the tub. She must allow fate to flow over her as water flows over a rock in the river. Any falsehood, any conscious manipulation, would break the flow.

The coffee was ready and she took a cup to the table. Pushing the papers aside, she set the coffee down. Then she turned and looked directly into the young man's face. "Well, Buddy," she said, "I guess I always knew you might show up when I least expected it."

Now something in his eyes did change. Edna let her breath out in a deep sigh, pushed the papers aside and began setting the table.

"Sit down, Buddy," she said once again and this time he moved into the dining area and took the place she had set for him. He open the can of beer and began to drink. His eyes left her for the first time.

Edna returned to her cooking. Her back to him, she began cutting up an onion and the potatoes. Once again the room filled with warm familiar smells.

"You want the cheese in your eggs?" she said.
"Yes, ma'am."

Now Edna was silent as she moved from one task to another. The biscuits were in the oven, the potatoes frying slowly on the back of the stove. She broke the eggs into a bowl and added some cheese. "Three going to be enough, Buddy?"

"Yes, ma'am. You got another beer?
"Don't know, Buddy. You can look. Hunt around in the back. I don't drink much beer." He didn't move.

"Supper'll be ready in another minute."

The biscuits were ready, and she scrambled the eggs and poured them into the frying pan. When they were done, she filled a plate.

"I don't think I'll eat right now, but I'll have a cup of coffee with you," she said. She took the plate and two coffees to the table and sat across from him. He began to eat, using the knife to push his food onto the fork. Edna drank her coffee.

"There's more biscuits. You want some more? I forgot to give you jelly with them."

Once again, "Yes, ma'am."

Edna brought the biscuits and preserves to the table, but this time she didn't sit down. Standing beside him she said, "You think you gonna spend the night, Buddy?"

There was a long pause. Then he said, "No. I gotta go, but I need money."

"Sure, Buddy. Sure, I should have known you'd need money. My bag's over there on the sofa. You can get it yourself. I'll just put some of the biscuits and cheese in a bag for you to take with you. I think I've got some cookies, too."

Once again Edna forced thought out of her mind. She concentrated wrapping the biscuits and never looked as he took her wallet from her pocket book and extracted the small amount of cash she had left from the week's shopping.

She heard rather than saw him step toward the wall phone near the desk. He was pulling on something. She saw it in his hand. He had pulled out the line from the phone to the jack and was looping it over his palm as he came toward her. She held out the package of food. This was the final test, Edna thought. He took the bag from her outstretched hand, his eyes searching her face as he had before when she first saw him though the steam.

"I'm going," he said. He turned and walked out the way he had come in. A moment later she heard her car start. Edna sat down at the table and stared vacantly at her coffee. The sound of the car descending the driveway was the only thing in her consciousness. When it was gone her mind was an absolute blank.

Suddenly a wave of nausea engulfed her. The coffee in her empty stomach turned to acid, and she bolted for the bathroom. Barely making it, Edna collapsed over the toilet bowl and began retching violently. Next to her Harold's huge tub was still full from the interrupted bath. When the heaving stopped she moved to its edge and plunged her face and hands into the tepid water. It was over.

Edna stood up unsteadily. Ignoring her glasses which she had knocked to the floor in her haste, she looked into the mirror at the drained face and wild hair. With a deep inhalation, she picked up a comb and began her reconstruction. When she could recognized the face before her, she turned slowly and walked into the bedroom to kneel beside the bed. The phone was just out of sight where she had kicked it. She dialed 911.

"This is Edna Rodgers at 732 Mountain Ridge Road. I've had an intruder. He just left driving a blue 1998 Ranger, Georgia tag number 973 RVB."

Tree reaching out to the sun

THE HIGHWAY

Let's get this straight from the beginning. This story is fiction. I have a brother, but he is younger than I am and lives in New Jersey. What's more, he is one of the most honorable men I have ever known. If anyone was a bully when we were kids, it was me.

The trip to Mobile is real enough. I've driven it several times, but never alone and never at night. But my teacher in ninth grade English class was a Miss Drumhouser.

The highway stretched out before me, 450 miles of asphalt with nothing but an occasional exit sign to break the monotony. I hate driving. Some people love cars and get a kick out of being behind a wheel. Not me!

Ordinarily, on a trip like this I would bring along a couple of books on tape to keep me entertained, but the phone call from my sister-in-law came after eight p.m., and there was no time to do anything other than gas up the car, grab a thermos of coffee to keep me awake, and go. It was winter; the sun was down, and I would have to drive the whole 450 miles in darkness.

My brother Bob's SUV had been T-boned by a truck as Bob came out of a side street. His internal organs were severely damaged, and it didn't look good. We weren't close, but hell. He was family. Bob and I still exchange Christmas cards, but that's about the extent of our relationship. Still, like I said, he's family. I was expected, and if it meant driving all night, well then, that's what I had to do.

Mobile was over seven hours away, a long, dull drive even in the daytime. Interstate 85 passed through both Atlanta and Montgomery, but for the most part it would be nothing but a divided highway the whole 450 miles—a boring, mesmerizing stretch of pavement with nothing to look at but a broken yellow line.

So far the trip hadn't been too bad. I'd made it through Atlanta in less than two hours, and there'd been enough cars on the road to keep me alert. The FM station came in clear enough, and I like classical music; but as I headed south toward Montgomery the station faded, and there was nothing but static. I shut it off. Surely I could withstand a few hours of my own company without coming apart at the seams. Just the same, I began to squirm. My back hurt. My butt was numb, and the bottom of my feet itched.

Bob was three years older than me and Mother's pride and joy. Sometimes I wonder why she bothered to have another kid. Mother loved men, all men, all ages, and she was good with them too. She knew how their minds worked and how to flatter them. I don't think she liked women very much. I suppose they were competition. Even at that, having a daughter might have been O.K. if I had been the right kind of daughter, one with whom she could share her seductive secrets. A daughter who would sit at her mother's knee and learn how to manipulate the male animal, but I wasn't interested.

I wasn't pretty. I wasn't seductive, and I didn't want to get ahead in life by appealing to the male ego. And then there was Bob himself. Bob was a bully, plain and simple. He knew how to charm Mother, but when charm didn't work; he had other talents. Ours was not a happy relationship. Now he was dying, might not even last the night. His wife said he was awake and not in a lot of pain; but he knew his injuries were probably fatal, and he was calling for me.

Why? Did he want forgiveness, or was this another way to bully me, make me jump through his hoops? And here I was, not jumping exactly, but driving in the dark, mad as hell, and jacked up on black coffee. The distance from Atlanta to Montgomery was over 150 miles, another two and a half to three hours driving before the black monotony of endless road was relieved by anything more than a passing car, and after Montgomery, the long haul to Mobile was several more hours of fighting sleep and boredom.

Just outside of Montgomery a trailer rig drew up behind me and leaned on the horn. Startled, I swerved to the right and over onto the corrugated asphalt put there to waken drifting drivers. I was awake all right, awake and cursing at the top of my lungs. The red of the guy's taillight disappeared into the distance. What is it the airline pilots say about their job? Something about hours of utter boredom punctuated by moments of stark terror.

The adrenalin began to wear off, and I was back to feeling bored and sorry for myself. This damned road would never end. I tried the radio again. Nothing but static from one end of the band to the other. Crap. I slammed my hand against the dash. The static sputtered and stopped. Crap, again. The clock on the radio went black. Apparently I'd killed the whole damned thing.

I checked my mileage for the millionth time. What was it last time I looked? Couldn't remember. Maybe the odometer was broken too. What about exit signs? Must check next time I passed one, but I didn't have a map and just knowing the exit number wouldn't do me any good.

"Mine eyes have seen the glory of the coming of the Lord."
It was the first song that came to mind, but singing didn't
help. The sound of my own voice echoing through the
empty car was worse than the steady click of the tires on
the roadbed.

Perhaps I could remember some of the poems I learned in
Miss Drumhouser's ninth grade English class. She'd been
the high school drama coach and believed in the value of
memorization.

> "Out of the night that covers me black as the pit from
> pole to pole, I thank whatever God may be for my
> unconquerable soul."

No-o-o, *Invictus* wouldn't do it, and I couldn't remember
anything else.

Falling back into silence, I twisted in my seat, jiggled my
arms and wobbled my knees. I pummeled the steering
wheel. Gees, I was uncomfortable. I yawned. I picked my
nose. I scratched my rump and nearly lost control of the car
doing so. This was purgatory.

And still the road went on. Outside there was nothing but
black. Inside, nothing but the sound of the engine and the
rhythmic thump of the tires on the road below. There
hadn't been an exit sign for what seemed like ages. In fact,
I was on some sort of bridge with high retaining walls on
either side. There was no way to stop, no way to get off the
road.

The thought hit me like ice. *It is purgatory!* That semi just
outside of Montgomery didn't miss me after all. I was dead
and didn't know it. My body is back there lying in the grass
beside the highway while the police waited for a crash

truck to take it away, and I'm going to spend eternity in this damned car, eternity in the dark with nothing but a yellow line disappearing into the distance through the windshield.

The whole picture was clear to me now. This was never going to end. The irony was perfect. Bob was going to recover. I was the one who would die. Then I saw the sign: "Mobile 20 miles."

The city of Mobile is situated on Mobile Bay and surrounded by swamp. The last 20 miles of Interstate 85 are elevated, built high over the mucky water and uncertain land around the city itself. It was almost dawn. I was there, and I was alive.

STIGMATA

Stigmata is a spontaneous manifestation of bloody wounds on a person's body similar to the wounds of the crucified Jesus. The blood will pour forth for an unknown amount of time and then just as suddenly disappear. The wounds do not infect, and the blood may have a sweet smell.

As light crept in through the small window high over her bed, Lucy awoke from a dreamless sleep, stretched, and turned over. As she opened her eyes she saw blood stains on her pillow and along the edge of the sheet where she had pulled it up to her chin. Started, she put her hands up to her face and smelled roses.

Lucy had lived in New York City all her life. She'd been a foster child, shuttled from one family to another during her early years, finally living in a group home with other foster children until she was old enough to get out on her own. All the families had been Catholic. She understood about stigmata. The nuns had made sure of it.

She lay absolutely still for a while, then took the edge of the sheet—she would have to wash it anyway—and carefully wiped the blood from her palms. Slowly the red drops reformed, oozing out through the unbroken skin.

Lucy folded back the bed covers and pulled up her nightgown. Apparently the bleeding on her side had just started. If she moved quickly she wouldn't have to launder everything. Well, she thought, it was plain that God had made a mistake, and as usual Lucy was the one who would have to clean up the mess.

She looked around the small room for something to staunch the blood. The band aids in the box she kept over the sink weren't big enough. A sink, her own source of running water in her own room, was a glorious luxury. She used it for everything, dishes, laundry, personal hygiene. A sink meant she didn't have to share kitchen facilities with the rest of the boarders. A sink gave her the autonomy she had lacked as a child. The toilet was down on the next floor. Still, Lucy felt immensely fortunate.

Lucy's room was in the attic of a row house in the Bronx, and the reason it had a sink was because a former occupant had used it as a photography studio. The room was dark, cramped and still smelled faintly of chemicals on damp days, but it was cheap, and unlike the rooms she'd had as a child, she shared it with no one.

Lucy hunted around for something to bind up her wounds. She settled on an old T-shirt and tore it into strips with her teeth. With quick movements she folded one of the strips and used the band aids to tape it to her side. She would have to wash the blood from the sheet and pillow case before she bandaged her hands.

As she rubbed the edge of the sheet under the tap, she thought about the day ahead of her. Today was the day she saw Mr. Kelly. This bleeding was just one more thing to cope with, one more problem in a world beset with problems. A doctor, even if she could afford one, would be of no use if the skin wasn't broken. And what would she tell a priest? Yes, Father. I have sinned, but I don't care.

The sheet was clean now, and she flipped it deftly over the back of her only chair. It would dry before she got home. She washed the pillow case and then wadded up the rest of the strips and tied them over her palms. There was a drug store on the corner. She would stop there on the way to work and pick up a roll of gauze and some tape, probably a couple of pairs of surgical gloves as well. There was no telling how long the bleeding would last.

Lucy was a small woman with dark hair and a plain face. Now in her early thirties, she still had the look of a street kid—strong, sinewy, and never fully in repose. Only her eyes showed anything of intelligence or grace.

Having had nothing as a child, Lucy needed little now. A room of her own, a job, a few books, and occasional boyfriend. There was no closet in the room. Hooks on one wall held the smocks she wore at work, a coat, and a couple of dresses. There were shelves for her few possessions. She had everything she needed

She made a cup of coffee on a hot plate and laced it liberally with canned milk from a small fridge. From a plastic bag on a shelf she extracted a roll saved from another meal. That and an apple would hold her till evening if necessary. She ate quickly and washed the cup.

Lucy brushed her teeth, straightened up the bed, and looked around her room with satisfaction. It was more like a cell than a bedroom, but a cell suited her—her sanctuary in a troubled world.
The owner of the house had expressed no interest in the old

photography equipment when Lucy moved in.

"It's all junk," she said leaning against the doorjamb. "Do whatever you want with it."

The projector was worthless. Lucy hauled it out to the trash, but there were several trays she could use for storage and two perfectly good photo flood lamps. On a whim, Lucy mounted the lamps high in opposing corners of the room. Over one she draped a yellow cloth, over the other a blue cloth. They now became the sun and the moon. It only took a flip of a switch.

Lucy dressed and prepared to leave. She would use the bathroom on her way out. Mr. Kelly lived across town and the unscheduled stop at the pharmacy would make her miss the subway if she didn't hurry.

Lucy called herself a professional caregiver. True, she'd never had any formal training and had never been licensed, but she'd been taking care of other people all her life. Foster children were expected to earn their keep. Actually, the state paid foster families to take these unwanted or unadaptable children off their hands; but it was a meager sum, and the families usually expected to get some work out of their charges. They became unpaid baby-sitters, or more often, caretakers for an elderly and somewhat demented family member.

Lucy developed a talent for handling difficult people. She was particularly good with cantankerous old men. She knew just when to play the stern nurse and when to play the flirtatious coquette. She got them to take their medicine, persuaded them to bathe, jollied them into shaving, and left them smiling. Nothing disgusted her. Nothing offended her.

She knew when to allow a pat and how to avoid a pinch. Lucy would take cases when others wouldn't. She stayed with families until their burdens passed on to whatever reward or punishment awaited them in the next life. Everyone said she was a saint. Now, she thought as she stood in line at the pharmacy, I have to pay for it with this damned bleeding.

She pushed her way onto a crowded subway and grabbed one of the overhead straps. The lump of bandage was annoying, but there was no other discomfort. Nothing hurt, but she would have to figure out a way to manage her tasks without making a mess.

Ed Kelly lived by himself in a federally sponsored high-rise. Unlike many of her former clients he was mobile, continent, and lucid, but he was a lonely complaining old man. He needed help with laundry, some light cleaning, and an errand or two run, but most of all he needed human companionship. Lucy was his only friend.

Nine o'clock and he was standing at the open door to his apartment as she stepped off the elevator.

"There you are girl. You're late."

"It's just nine, Mr. Kelly, but it's nice to know you are waiting for me. Makes a girl feel wanted."

"Humph. Just waiting for my paper, girl."

Lucy scooted through the opening, neatly avoiding a slap on the bottom. The apartment was a mess, magazines and papers strewn across the floor, dishes encrusted with food on top of the television set, dirty clothes everywhere. Lucy began picking up things as she walked across the room to the kitchen area. Dishes in the sink, clothes in a pile, the papers folded, no wasted motion. Lucy took pride in her efficiency.

Mr. Kelly settled in his overstuffed chair and watched her work with a look of satisfaction on his face.

"Have you had a good week, Mr. Kelly? I see the Yankees lost again the other day."

Lucy knew this comment would release a long monologue on the stupidity of the team's management, the perfidiousness of its players, and the blind, dumb luck of their opponents. All Lucy had to do was nod, and mutter an occasional, "Really" or "Oh, yes. I'm sure." Meanwhile, the room began to take on a semblance of order.

Not every client required this degree of deference. On alternate days Lucy cared for Joe McFarland. Mr. McFarland suffered a debilitating stroke at the age of fifty-five. Lucy was more than his care give Lucy was his drinking buddy and all around party girl—as much of a party girl as a crippled and aphasic man could manage.

Less than two years ago Joe McFarland was a marine recruiter flashing his metals and telling war stories to college students around the Northeast. Today he was unable to walk without assistance, unable to speak more than a few words, and dependent on his wife for almost everything—his wife and Lucy.

Mrs. McFarland was a pretty women almost fifteen years Joe's junior. She hadn't bargained for this. Her once burly marine had become a burdensome child, and she treated him as such.

44

"Lucy's coming today, Sweetheart, and she'll take you for a nice little walk in the park. We're looking forward to Lucy, aren't we, Sweetheart? We always have such a good time with her, don't we?"

The poor woman's desperation was palpable. Lucy was hardly through the door before she made her escape.

"I'll be home at six, Lucy. See that he stays bundled up." And she was gone.

The change in Lucy was immediate. Her posture relaxed, her vocabulary coarsened, her demeanor became playful, even provocative. Mr. McFarland was now Joe, her Joe. She told him stories. She made up games. She flirted and shared secrets with him. Their walks in the park became visits to a local bar where the small dark women and the crippled marine were welcomed as regulars.

"Hey, Lucy, Joe. What will you have? I'm buying today."

"Joe and I will have a couple of Buds. Make it draft, Benny. None of that piss in a bottle. Where do you want to sit, Joe?"

Joe would gesture to a place away from the TV knowing that Lucy would draw attention from the tube and onto the two of them. .She radiated a sexual energy that connected with every man in the room, but Joe was the only man she looked at. She never left his side. The regulars joked and flirted but went no further. It was understood Lucy belong to Joe.

For Lucy it was a job. For Joe it was a lifeline, the only solace in an existence that had turned sour.

Lucy would see Joe tomorrow. Today Mr. Kelly commanded her complete attention. She pulled on a pair of yellow Rubbermaid gloves and began to wash the dishes. The bulky bandages made her movements awkward. One of the dishes slipped out of her hand and clattered against the porcelain.

"Jesus Christ. You Goddamn twit. Can't you do anything right?"

"I beg your pardon."

"I said, 'You Goddamn twit. Can't you do anything right?'"

Mr. Kelly must have thought she hadn't heard him the first time. It was a bit much even for Lucy. She turned, scooped up the pile of dirty clothes and took it into the bedroom. She would finish the dishes later. She stripped the unmade bed and added the linen to her growing pile. Mr. Kelly was now standing in the door. He loved to watch her work. Lucy tossed a pillow at him.

"Here you old reprobate. Pull the pillow case off for me so I can put it in the wash."

Mr. Kelly dropped the pillow on the floor, turned, and left the room. The next thing Lucy heard was talk radio blaring from the next room. A strident voice was trashing the liberal media and cursing crooks in Washington. Lucy could hear Mr. Kelly chuckle as she took the laundry into the bathroom and began checking the pockets for handkerchiefs.

Mr. Kelly's handkerchiefs were always a mess, gray and covered with bloody snot. Mr. Kelly disdained Kleenex. Apparently tissues were for wimps no matter what the state of one's sinuses. She couldn't put the handkerchiefs into the wash until she had soaked them and scraped away the detritus. She poured a little Clorox over the wads of cloth and immersed them in hot water.

Lucy got down on her knees and cleaned the bottom of the shower stall. Mr. Kelly was a square, heavy-set man with a red face and a lot of body hair. The drain was almost completely clogged. Next the toilet. At least Mr. Kelly had flushed. Sometimes he didn't.

Lucy returned to the handkerchiefs, scrubbed away the now softened snot, squeezed them out, and added them to the pile of laundry. That done, she stripped off the rubber gloves and examined the bandages. The bleeding had almost stopped. The smell of roses was gone. She replaced the heavy strips of cloth with squares of gauze and taped them securely in place, then pulling the bathroom door closed, she checked her side. There was nothing there at all now.

"I'm going down to the basement now, Mr. Kelly."

"And I'm coming with you to make sure you don't dawdle away the time jabbering with the other flibbedy-jibbets down there."

"Fine, Mr. Kelly. Bring the paper, and I'll read to you."

Mr. Kelly had the *New York Times* delivered to his door every morning, but his eyes were going bad. He needed a magnifying glass to read anything smaller than the headlines. Hating any display of weakness, he surreptitiously slid the glasses behind the cushions of his chair any time Lucy was into the room. Lucy noticed his little sleight of hand shortly after she started working for him and began to look for excuses to read to him.

She shared Mr. Kelly's passion for the *Times* It was her eye on the world, her source of social insight, her avenue to contemporary art and science, but paying for a newspaper was not in her budget. Reading to Mr. Kelly was as much of a reward for her services as her salary, and she could usually find some pretext for it.

She hid her enthusiasm as they descended to the laundry room. They were in luck. The place was deserted. Mr. Kelly could denigrate the paper and its lackeys all he liked. Once again, little was required on her part. Mr. Kelly made himself comfortable while Lucy stuffed the laundry, detergent, and quarters into the waiting machines. Then she settled herself and began to read.

The machines swished and vibrated. The dryers hummed. Lucy's voice rose and fell as Mr. Kelly found fault with the reporters, the editors, the columnists, and men and women who wrote letters to the opinion page. In a small damp room two floors below ground, two contented people passed a comfortable morning.

"Mr. Kelly, it is almost one o'clock. What do you want me to do about your lunch? I could make an omelet if you still have any eggs."

"If you think I'm going to eat that slop you prepare, you are sadly mistaken." This meant Mr. Kelly was taking her out to lunch. It was turning out to be a rather good day after all.

"Very well, Mr. Kelly. I'll finish the dishes, and we can go."

Ten minutes later, seated in a corner booth at a nearby Italian cafe, Lucy and Mr. Kelly could have passed for an old married couple.

"See that you don't order anything over five dollars—and be sure to wipe the silverware. These Wops leave all kinds of crud on their forks."

Lucy looked at the menu. She had been given so little choice in her life she was nearly incapable of making one when the opportunity arose. As a child she was fortunate if her foster family sent her off to school with anything to eat at all. When one of her foster mothers asked if she wanted cheese or peanut butter in her sandwich, she'd been unable to answer.

"What's the matter with you, child? Speak up. Are you stupid or something?"

The words rang in her ears even now. She simply said, "I'll have whatever you are having, Mr. Kelly." They ate in silence. If Mr. Kelly noticed the tape around her palms, he said nothing.

Lucy was used to eating by herself. A silent meal was an opportunity to read or think, or simply observe her surroundings. She focused on a couple across the room who were arguing, oblivious to the fact that others were listening to them.

Who needs TV thought Lucy. Eavesdropping is cheaper and more entertaining. She followed their angry voices for a while, then lost interest and began to monitor the coming and going of the waiters. The one across the room was obviously new. A rotund little man, he was awkward and easily confused. The other waiters were obliged to cover for his mistakes.

He must be a relative of one of the owners, thought Lucy Why else were the rest of the waiters so tolerant of his ineptitude. "He'll drop a plate before we leave," she thought to herself. Lucy watched for a while, but he made her nervous; and she shifted her gaze once more. Mr. Kelly was finishing his spaghetti.

"Take the rest of the bread." he commanded. "And the butter too. It's paid for. No point leaving it. Go ahead. Wrap it up in your napkin like a good girl." Lucy did as she was told.

Once back at the apartment, he'd most likely tell her to, "...throw the damned Dago bread out." Lucy had learned to keep a plastic baggy in her pocket for such largess. One more thing she didn't have to buy.

Lucy returned to her tasks. Mr. Kelly seemed more edgy than usual. As it neared five o'clock he began pacing around and mumbling to himself. Finally he faced her.

"You know, girl, you play your cards right and I just might marry you and leave you all my money."

Lucy laughed, "What, and be your unpaid maid? I've been used for free most of my life. No thanks. I like you fine, Mr. Kelly." She smiled at him with genuine affection. "But no thanks."

Mr. Kelly was standing close to her now. He reached out and grabbed her by the wrists.

"What's going on with these bandages, girl?" he asked. What have you done to yourself?" She stared at him, and he let go.

She held her palms out toward him as if she was receiving a heavy platter. As she did the blood renewed its flow and soaked through the protective gauze. As the bandages reddened, all color drained from Mr. Kelly's ruddy face.

"Jesus Christ!" he said. "Jesus Christ. What have you done?"

He continued to stare, then shook his head. "Can't you take better fucking care of yourself than that?"

"Good bye, Mr. Kelly. I'll see you day after tomorrow."

"Stupid girl," she heard him mumble as the door closed. "Poor stupid, girl."

The elevator was at the end of the hall. By the time she reached it, any thought of Mr. Kelly had washed away like a wave receding from a beach. She pushed the button, and the doors opened. She entered, and they closed. The only thing on her mind now was a simple room where she controlled the heavens with a flip of a switch.

THE SHORT STORY

*I've changed the name of the
artist and her family. Otherwise
this story is absolutely true
and haunts me to this day.*

The door opened, and a couple peered hesitantly into the room. "We're the Baines," the woman said. "We've come a long way to see this exhibit."

They were not exactly old, maybe their late fifties, but they had the look that elderly people get when they've lived together for a long time: comfortable, well worn, and just a little sad.

"I hope we're not intruding," said the man, but of course they were, and we all knew it. Just the same we smiled and welcomed them. "Come in," we murmured. "Please come in." It was after all a public room in a public building.

We were in the community room at the local library where we met every Friday at ten. This morning the Clarkesville Writing Group was discussing the dynamics of the short story. We're an informal group, and our number varies from week to week. Today there were only six of us.

The community room is spacious, but it lacks windows and it is gray: grayish carpeting on the floor, utilitarian blue gray seats on the chrome chairs, and a knobby gray wall covering on which hung an ever changing display of charts, photos, children's drawings—whatever the library or the community wants to exhibit.

Today the room housed an art show. One look was all that was needed to realize the show covered a wide range of talent. Some of the paintings were colorful but decidedly amateur. Some were trite little still-lives. The best of the lot were landscapes and among them hung several lovely paintings of rocks, sand, and sea.

The couple apologized again for the interruption and added that they had driven from all the way from Mississippi to see their daughter's paintings. The aspiring writers made a few more polite remarks, just enough to let the Baines know we were not too put out by the intrusion but really wanted to get back to the subject at hand.

The Baines walked to the far end of the room and focused on several paintings of bottles, plates of fruit, and other inanimate objects, the sort of exercise a beginner might undertake. They were well rendered but static. "These are some of the first paintings our daughter ever did," Mrs. Baine said. "She painted ever since she was a child."

"We've kept the best ones at home," the husband added.

"These," Mrs. Baine said moving to several of the seascapes, "were done when she was in Hawaii." The difference was striking. They were beautiful. Painting moving water is difficult, and capturing surf, sand, and sky without being maudlin is an accomplishment for any artist. The light from the seascapes spread over the gray walls and changed the character of the room. No longer stark and utilitarian, it somehow became a warmer more welcoming space. The room itself became younger.

The couple looked about a little more, but it was still awkward. Obviously we couldn't return to our literary discussion in their presence. Everybody made a few more courteous remarks, and the Baines again stood looking displaced and hesitant. I think we were all getting the same uneasy feeling. Everything the Baines said was in the past tense.

Finally, pausing at the door Mrs. Baine thanked us once more and repeated the words they had said upon entering: "We've come such a very long way. You see," she added, "we had to make sure our daughter had a proper headstone. Her husband refuses to do it."

Then they left, and our attention shifted from the walls to the six of us sitting around folding tables in the center of the room. Our leader picked up where she had left off. "In addition to a plot," she read from her text, "a short story must have a recognizable beginning, middle, and end.

Later when I went out into the main library, I noticed the sign in the hall: "This exhibit is in memory of Martha Baine Cunningham."

A WOMAN IN LOVE

Newsweek Magazine **did publish an issue that promised**
"The secrets of the Universe" on its cover. I'm a sucker
for this sort of thing and read the article over several
times without learning much of anything, but the idea of
multi-universes intrigued me.

That and my fondness for interesting luncheon
companions resulted in the story of a middle-aged woman
who suddenly finds herself in love.

Rebecca awoke slowly and with a feeling of deep
contentment. Light streamed through a window beside her
bed. Somewhere a bird chirped. She rolled over and
indulged in a long languid stretch. I'm in love, she thought.

The shock brought her fully awake. She was middle-aged,
slightly overweight, a widow for over ten years, and there'd
been no one in her life since Bob died. She didn't even
have a male friend.

This year Valentine's Day had fallen on a Saturday. Ads
for roses, restaurants specials, and weekend getaways were
everywhere. The local newspaper even ran a contest to
name the community's most romantic man. That must be it,
she thought. All that commercial hoopla, it's invaded my
dreams.

Rebecca got out of bed, showered, and prepared for the day
still puzzled by her mood. She caught herself smiling for no
reason. She started to waltz around the room as she dressed.

She stopped dead, amazed at her own behavior. The feeling wore off as the day progressed. When she got ready to go to bed that night she wondered vaguely if she'd have another dream, one that would explain her emotional jag of that morning.

There was no dream, at least not one she could remember, but she awoke with the same strange feeling, a feeling that was sweet and almost giddy. Something wonderful had come into her life. Rebecca didn't read romantic novels. Even as a young woman, she'd never fanaticized over movie stars or handsome men at work. She tried to remember what she had dreamed, and came up with a blank. She remembered feeling happy but couldn't remember why.

The next morning was a repeat of the day before, except that this morning it was raining. Rebecca listened to the sound of the raindrops as they pattered against the windowpane and whispered through the leaves, and thought about fireplaces, hot toddies and cuddling up on the sofa under Grandma's old quilt. Her apartment didn't have a fireplace, Rebecca never drank alone, and her Grandmother didn't know how to sew. What the bleep was going on.

That afternoon Rebecca was pushing her cart down the isle of a local grocery store and ran into a friend she hadn't seen for a while. They exchanged the usual pleasantries.

"It's been a long time."

"Yes, it has. How are you doing?"

"Fine. Fine. Just a little older."

"Not you, Rebecca. You look younger than you did five years ago. In fact, you're radiant. What's your secret?"

"No secret," she said uncomfortably and looked for an opportunity to get away. Later the same day when someone else commented on her appearance, she had to admit to herself something had happened. She actually felt younger.

The next day was Saturday, the day she had lunch with three of her women friends. She was running late. As she approached the table her companions began to kid her. "Had a hot date last night?" This was from Nancy Johnson, seated in the far corner of the booth. Nancy had known Rebecca the longest. They'd been friends since high school, went to the same college and were in each other's weddings. "As close as sisters," they often said.

"Oh my gosh, Look at her blush," said Cynthia who sat next to Nancy. Cynthia Crosby was a retired high school science teacher and looked every inch the part—frameless glasses, conservative suit, and sturdy shoes—Cynthia was the voice of reason in every argument.

"Rebecca... has... a... boy-friend," Janie chanted in a singsong voice. Janie had been the class cut up. She was a bit of a know-it-all but well-meaning and a loyal friend. As Rebecca began to slide into the vacant space beside Janie, Janie tried to put her arm around her. Rebecca pulled away, obviously irritated.

"I do not have a boyfriend," Rebecca said sternly as she placed her purse on floor beside her seat. She was visibly upset. "I don't know why you're all saying that."

"All right." Janie patted Rebecca's hand. "Be that way. We'll wait."

"No, honest. I'm not seeing anyone. I haven't had a date in years. I don't know what you all are talking about," she said now firmly seated in the booth.

"Okay," said Nancy. "We'll change the subject."

The four women met for lunch on a regular basis. They were all educated, independent, progressive women. They gossiped like any other group of woman, but their conversations were usually more far reaching.

Nancy took the lead. "Did anyone read the most recent *Newsweek* magazine?"

"The one advertising 'The Secrets of The Universe'?" Cynthia said. "I'm surprised at *Newsweek*. The cover was more tabloid than international news. "

Nancy nodded. "Not only does it promise the secrets of this universe, it suggests there are more than just this one universe—multiverses they call them. I find that a little difficult to even imagine."

"I don't know why," Janie said brightly. "Once we thought the sun circled around the earth. Then we discovered the earth wasn't the center of everything after all, just one planet in our particular solar system. Then we learned that there were other suns and other solar systems circling around the center of a black hole in the middle of our galaxy. Pretty soon we find other galaxies out there, and who know what they're circling round, so it doesn't seem so strange that they're grouped together into one of many other universes... or is it universi?" Janie smiled and took a sip of her wine.

"Universe is singular," Cynthia said emphatically. She placed both her hands flat on the table and continued. "It refers to the totality of everything. The idea of a multi-universe is simply a mathematical quirk. It has to do with quantum physics. It's purely theoretical."

"We can see the other stars and the other galaxies," she continued. "We have tangible measurements ... physical proof. This multi-universe thing is like string theory. It's something scientists play around with. They've even suggested we may all have duplicates of ourselves, living in these other universes, other Janies, Nancys, and Rebeccas, like us but living out different mathematical realities."

She paused, sat back, and then added disdainfully, "The next thing you know someone will come up with the idea people can travel from one of these universes to another."

Nancy laughed. "I like the idea. Maybe I could take a lover in another galaxy and Don wouldn't mind because the me that was living here in this galaxy would go on being faithful to him alone."

This was when Rebecca snapped out of her reverie. "What?" she said and knocked over the glass of water the waiter had just put beside her plate. In the bustle that followed Rebecca was able to excuse herself and go to the restroom to dry off. By the time she got back everyone was talking about something else.

That night, back in her apartment Rebecca was unable to read and wandered around aimlessly wondering if it was too early to go to bed. This is silly, she scolded herself. She couldn't let go of the conversation at lunch. She'd even looked for the May 28th copy of *Newsweek* on the way home, but it wasn't on the newsstands anymore. Tomorrow she would go to the library and read it there.

Finally she gave up. If you can't beat them, join them, she thought. I'm going to pretend that I do have a lover from another dimension. She took a hot bath, sprayed her wrists with perfume, and put on her best nightgown. "All right, whoever you are, I'm ready," and she crawled into bed.

That night she did dream, but in the morning all she could remember was warmth and happiness. There had been someone there, but she didn't remember anything about him. Or her. I suppose it could be a her, she thought. But there was nothing, nothing at all ... nothing physical, nothing she could give a name to, just the giddy feeling of being in love.

Rebecca wasn't a scientist, but she'd read about the latest brain research in various magazine articles. Apparently emotions came from specific parts of the brain while rational thought came from a different place.

Love isn't rational. It's like politics and religion, she thought. *Scientific American* had recently carried a piece on the search for the God spot, the place in the brain that lights up in an MRI when an individual is engaged in prayer or meditation.

She remembered a bumper sticker that read, "God is Love." Rebecca wasn't particularly religious, but it annoyed her that some opportunist had summed up years of spiritual research and writing in something so simplistic. On the other hand maybe her right parietal lobe was causing her crazy feeling. Perhaps it was a tumor. Should she see a neurologist?

Whatever was going on, it wasn't normal, and she would have to do something about it. She picked up the phone and called Nancy who answered on the second ring. "I've got to talk to someone," Rebecca said.

"I knew it," replied Nancy. Tell Mama," and Rebecca could hear gleeful anticipation in her friend's voice. "It's about time you broke out of your shell and had a fling."

"No, no, no!" she fairly screamed into the phone. "I don't have a boyfriend, at least not one I can see and touch.

"Nancy," she moaned, "I think I'm going crazy."

Talking to Nancy did help a little. At least she was talking instead of obsessing about her weird feelings in private. The next time the four women had lunch together, it was Rebecca who brought up the subject of visitors from another dimension.

"I've never believed in aliens, but I've been having this strange feeling of a presence in my life. It's kind of nice. You know ... comforting. You remember the last time we met and you all kidded me about being in love? Well, I guess I am ... sort of. I told Nancy about it and she said maybe it was Bob's spirit, but that's silly. He's been gone over ten years."

"I don't know why that's silly," Janie said. "Time doesn't change things like that. He was your husband ... still is your husband, and maybe he's trying to contact you."

"Come on, Janie," Cynthia said. "Nobody here believes in 'ghosties, and ghoulies, and things that go bump in the night.'" She turned to Rebecca. "You don't really think you're being visited by Bob's ghost, do you Rebecca?"

61

"No," said Rebecca. "I hadn't thought about that, but even if I had, this isn't Bob. It's nothing like what we had together. Bob was my rock, my compass, my best friend, but our relationship wasn't at all sentimental or romantic. I loved him deeply, but I wasn't exactly 'in love' with him. You know what I mean."

"No, I don't know what you mean. " Janie was almost indignant. "You were married to him for fifteen years. You had two kids. You were devastated when he died. How can you say you weren't in love with him?"

"Easy," said Cynthia. "You're a romantic, Janie. You've had three husbands, three divorces, and goodness know how many flings. You fall in love at the drop of a hat, but some people are different."

"Enough," said Nancy. "This is serious. Rebecca is afraid she's going nuts. I don't know why. It sounds like fun to me. In fact, I'm a little jealous."

"Well, I'm just afraid there's something wrong. This isn't natural. I wake up with this feeling that something wonderful is about to happen. I can fly. I'm not just singing in the shower, I'm dancing around the house and skipping down the street."

"Enjoy it," said Cynthia. "I'm with Nancy. I'm jealous. You even look years younger. If you really feel there's something wrong, if you think it's a hormonal imbalance or something, call your doctor and get a complete physical." Three days later, Rebecca was back on the phone with Nancy. "I felt like a fool, Nancy." The doctor examined me, did blood work and everything else. There's nothing wrong with me. He kept asking what hurt. Why was I there? And what could I say? That I'm in love? I tried to describe what was happening, that I was feeling ridiculously happy ... almost child-like, and he said that if I was depressed he could prescribe something, but he'd never had anyone come in saying they were too happy."

"You are happy, aren't you Rebecca? I mean I can't really tell. One minute you're saying you're happy, and the next you're saying something's wrong. Is it sexual? Maybe it is a hormonal imbalance. Are you having ... err, orgasms in your sleep?

"I don't think so. I just feel good all over ... Oh! I don't remember," she wailed. "I feel a presence but not a person. Do you think it is God? I mean if God is love, maybe I'm having some sort of spiritual experience. What should I do? See a priest?"

"You can't. You're not Catholic."

"Well, maybe it is a tumor."

"Get a CAT scan. Did the doctor do a CAT scan?

"No."

"Then get one."

Friday rolled around again. The four women were in a booth at Harington's, another trendy restaurant in the suburbs. This time there was no hesitation. They all wanted to talk about Rebecca's disembodied romance.

"Does it happen every night?" Janie asked eagerly.

"I can't really tell you," Rebecca replied, "because I don't remember much. I just wake up feeling warm and contented ... and really, really, happy."

"But she insists it isn't sexual," Nancy said, "So it can't be an incubus."

"An incubus?" said Janie. "I thought an incubus was a demon of some sort."

"It is," said Cynthia. "Legend says they lie on top of a woman when she is sleeping. One version of the King Arthur myth says the wizard Merlin was sired by an incubus."

"Oh boy," said Janie, "This is getting better and better. Watch out Rebecca. You may wind up pregnant with Rosemary's Baby."

"All kidding aside, Rebecca's worried that there may be something wrong with her," said Nancy. She's seen a doctor, and he can't find anything physical. Maybe she should see a shrink."

"Good idea," said Janie. "I saw a therapist after my last divorce. She helped a lot. I was dating again in two months."

"Janie, dear. Shut up," said Nancy. "I'm not sure Rebecca wants to be 'cured.' Do you, Rebecca? Do you want this to go away?"

Before Rebecca could answer, Cynthia interrupted. "There's one more thing you should consider before you do anything, Rebecca," she said. "It's from Roman mythology—the story of Cupid and Psyche."

Cynthia continued. "Psyche was fair of face and form, so lovely and innocent that Venus, the goddess of love and beauty, became jealous. She called her son Cupid to her side and demanded that he wound Psyche with one of his arrows and make her fall in love with a hideous monster.

"Cupid goes to do his mother's bidding, but when he sees how beautiful Psyche is, he becomes distracted and nicks himself with his own arrow. Now he is in love with Psyche, and to protect her from his mother he whisks her away to a magnificent castle where she has everything she needs. There Cupid visits her in the dark of night. He tells her she must never try to look at him.

Psyche's sisters learn of this and convince Psyche that her unseen husband is a demon. They tell her to light a candle and find out who is in her bed. She does as they suggest, but when she finds that her lover is the most beautiful man she has ever seen, she is so overwhelmed with love that she let a drop of hot wax fall on his naked shoulder. Cupid awakes and promptly disappears, never to return.

And so there you have it dear readers, what is your opinion? Did Rebecca have a brain tumor? Was God speaking to her? Did she have a lover from another dimension? And what would you do in her position?

Professor Wilson

JULIA

Who first said, "History is written by the victors"?
Winston Churchill? Niccolo Machiavelli?
Clausewitz? Herodotus?

How far back in the past do you want to go? In this story
two historians decide to reach into the future to find
answers. My inspiration for the telling came from
Julian Barnes who is not a historian at all, but an
acclaimed British novelist. In THE SENSE OF AN
ENDING he wrote:

"History is that certainty produced at the point where the
imperfections of memory meet the inadequacies of
documentation."

NASA SPACE LAB
DIVISION OF HUMAN HIBERNATION AND
CRYOGENICS
2060

"Julia ... Julia." Nothing.

A few minutes later: "Julia, it's time to wake up. The
woman's voice was soft ... persuasive.

Julia heard, but made no response.

The voice was still gentle but more insistent. "Julia. Julia,
you need to wake up now."

"I hear you."

"Open your eyes, Julia."

"I'm not ready."

"O.K. Just listen to my voice. I need you to wake up."

Julia felt a hand on her cheek. She tried to move away, but couldn't. Fingers slid down her arm and touched her palm. "Squeeze my hand if you can feel this." Julia complied.

"Good. Good girl. Now tell me your name."

"Julia Madison."

"Good girl. Can you tell me anymore?"

"Doctor Julia Madison." There was a note if irritation.

"Very good," the voice said close to her head. Then it became a little louder and seemed to turn and speak to a third party somewhere in the room. "I think she is going to be fine." The hand kept stroking her arm.

"Julia, she said, do you remember any more?"

"I volunteered for this."

"You did, Julia, and you will go down in history because of it."

"History is just one damned thing after another," Julia replied.

Julia was sitting on a bench in the spring sunshine. She was
playing hooky. Her dissertation could wait. Professor
Wilson could wait. Not only was she the brightest and the
best of the new grad students, she was pretty sure the good
professor had a crush on her.

Julia had always been the brightest and the best. Straight
As, graduated from high school at fifteen, majored in
science and technology at the University of California,
Berkeley, became interested in human behavior and was
presently working on her Ph.D. in history at Harvard. Now
the warm spring day was making her philosophical.

"What's the point," she mused to herself. "Why learn all
this stuff and then have it blown away by politics? In the
end, we don't know anything for sure. The winners write
the history books. Then the politicians take over and twist it
into whatever knot best serves their needs."

She closed her eyes and turned her face up to the sun. The
light coming through her lids was still strong. She was
trying to describe its exact color when a shadow fell over
her and a voice said, "Ms. Madison. You're supposed to be
in the lab this afternoon."

"Think of the devil and he's sure to appear," she said
without opening her eyes. "You don't really need me today,
do you Professor Wilson?"

"I guess not," he said, and sat down beside her.

And that's the way it began. They were kindred spirits.
John Wilson, the brilliant historian and Julia Madison, his

equally brilliant assistant. He was forty-two, ambitious, and already well-established in the field of political history. She was mercurial, flirtatious, one of the youngest Ph.D. candidates at the university, and very, very sure of herself.

They sat in companionable silence in the warm sunshine, the pretty young girl and the handsome older man, neither one anxious to break the spell of warmth and sunshine. After a while he reached for her hand and said, "Come on, we need something cool to drink."

He led her to one of the local pubs near the university. They sat a back booth, one of the many dark places enjoyed by the students when they wanted privacy with their brew. They talked for two hours. They'd read the same books, shared the same political philosophy, and liked the same music. Perfect soul mates except for one problem.

Professor Wilson looked at his watch and said, "I've got to go. Have to take my son to soccer practice. See you in the lab." He went to the bar, paid the bill, and walked out into the sunshine.

"Hm", thought Julia. Good father, bad husband, and she got up to go. The next day it rained.

For two weeks they worked in the lab, their paths crossing and crisscrossing with no more than a nod. Then Julia took things into her own hands. She sought him out in his office. When he stood up, she pushed the door closed behind her. He didn't seem surprised. She walked across the room, put her arms around him and kissed him. He broke the kiss and went to the door, locked it and turned, beckoning her back into their embrace. He'd been waiting for her.

For the next two weeks they met regularly. His office was located at the end of a hall on the fourth floor but there was still a certain amount of traffic. "If we continue like this," Julia said, "we're sure to be discovered. It's time to get a room."

"I like this," Julia said as she walked around a king-sized bed at a Motel Six north of the campus. "Your office couch is nice but does present certain limitations."

"It may indeed, Ms. Madison. Why don't you demonstrate the alternatives?"

"Glad to Professor Wilson," she laughed and pushed him backward onto the bed. He liked her to take the initiative. Whether it was sex or conversation, he always seemed to wait for the other person to make the first move—a consummate chess player who always chose black.

Lovemaking came easy, but their verbal duels were equally important to them both. Post-coital dialogue was as much Julia's task as the initial seduction. But once he got started, John Wilson would banter with her for hours. Julia searched for an opening.

"John, you know very well that history is really just one damned thing after another."

"Stop it, Julia," he said.

"Stop what, John?" she asked sweetly.

"Damn it, you know what."

"You want me to stop this?" and she slipped her hand under the covers.

"Stop quoting second-rate philosophers."

"Good God, John," she said turning over on her stomach. "What are you saying? Toynbee is the most renowned historian of our time." She knew that would provoke an argument.

"Historian, maybe, but he is a second-rate philosopher."

"Who would you prefer?

Dr. Wilson propped himself up on his elbow and began to expound while Julia basked in the warm glow of her conquest

John Wilson was a cynic. He would encourage a student to immerse himself—or herself since the majority of his students were women—in the works of a specific historian, to commit to that individual's political philosophy, and then just when the student thought he or she had discovered a real nugget of truth behind the flow of history, Wilson would take delight in pricking holes in the student's insights.

"Yes. Yes," he would say. "I think you have grasped the author's perspective rather well, but read ..." and then he would mention another historian's work, "and you'll find that its all nonsense."

Wilson was a popular teacher nonetheless. He was a handsome man, well built, his dark hair already turning a bit gray at the temples. He eyes were dark, too. He had the look of a highwayman in some old, romantic novel. On occasion, his pretty wife was seen around the campus, but she never entered the history department. She probably knew his reputation with women students and chose to turn a blind eye, which meant not showing up at his office announced or otherwise. And John *was* a good father to his three sons, participating in their soccer games and other school activities. If Julia ever felt any qualms about their affair, she could reassure herself that she in no way jeopardized his family.

Actually, she never gave it a second thought. As his graduate assistant she spent her days in his company and traveled with him for out-of-town speaking engagements. In the lab, their shouting matches were famous. Julia was the only one who stood up to him. John Wilson was a voracious reader, but Julia was the one with the photographic memory. John formulated theory, but Julia could and would correct him on facts.

If it pricked his ego, well ... she would make up for that when they were alone. After she completed her dissertation and began receiving job offers from history departments around the country, she turned them all down and stayed on as Wilson's assistant. Julia was in love.

They bantered about everything: the state of the world, the World Series, religion, how to make a good omelet, but mostly about human behavior and politics.

"Man is simply not a rational animal so how is one to come up with a rational explanation for any historical event?" Julia said.

"One can't, of course," Wilson replied, "Everything is a matter of perspective."

"But John, perspective is dependent on mood and moment. What is the mood of the people at any given time? What is the mood of the leaders?" said Julia. "That's what defines history."

"Better you should ask, what is the mood of the men who are writing the history books?"

"We do, John, or at least we try to, but you can read two historians writing about the same period of time and get two different descriptions of what's happening. You'd think the facts would be the same, but often there's no way to know which description is correct."

"So you look around," said Wilson, "and see if you can find more material, a third history book, a biography, military reports, weather reports, whatever. Don't be snide, Julia. It's our profession you're attacking."

"That's what I mean. 'History is just one damned thing after another.' She was quiet for a moment. Finally she turned to him and said, "Why don't you like Toynbee, John? He wasn't a leading international affairs specialist during two world wars for nothing."

"For God's sake, Julia. He was never sure about what he believed. He flip-flopped on all his political positions. He even allowed Hitler to convince him German expansion didn't threaten England."

"And he married his research assistant," Julia said.

There it was. Julia wanted to be his wife. For all his brilliance, John Wilson hadn't prepared for this, and he had no intention of threatening his comfortable domestic situation.

However, Julia said no more, and their relationship continued. Julia Madison with her rational mind and her prodigious memory was the perfect foil for John Wilson's creative nature and far reaching interests.

They were in the midst of one of their many debates. Julia prodded him to explain how any historian could be believed.

"How do you separate fact from perception, John? Historical theory is developed by individuals, and individuals can't escape their upbringing and their culture. They will always be swayed by emotions. They see what they're taught to see just like everyone else."

"That's a blanket statement if ever I heard one, Julia. You're saying that all history is biased?"

"I am."

"And you, Julia. Are you biased?"

"It's not bias if it's based on facts. Facts, facts, facts," she said pounding her fist into the palm of her other hand."

"But the historian chooses his facts based on his bias, and then weights them based on his emotional and cultural make up. You can't escape it Julia." He shrugged his shoulders. "That's why you have to keep reading, keep digging."

That stopped her for a while. She sat sulking and fiddling with a lock of her hair. Finally she said, "Too bad we can't bring some of those great historians back from the past, turn them loose in today's society, then see what happens to their the theories."

"Nice try, Julia. Time travel. How about sending one of our historians into the future to give people a firsthand report about our culture from someone who lived it?"

"You're being facetious," Julia snapped. He was angling for another battle of wits. They both knew the game. They thrived on it.

The affair continued for the next year and a half. John Wilson's wife, if not oblivious, seemed happy enough to say at home with her three boys. Julia was happy reigning over the history department and accompanying the professor when he went out of town for a speaking engagement. And John? John had the best of both worlds.

However, historians, of all people, should know conditions change with time. John's boys were growing up and becoming more independent. John's wife was becoming restless and wanted more of his time. Then John received an invitation for a speaking engagement in Europe.

"John, dear," his wife said, "this would be the perfect time to take that second honeymoon you've been promising me."

About the same time, Julia brought up Arnold Toynbee again. "John, dear," she said, "we have such a great working relationship, and even after two years sex is just as exciting as it ever was. We really should be married. You wouldn't be the first historian to divorce his wife and wed his assistant."

Caught between the two women, John took the coward's way out and turned down the speaking engagement with the excuse that he was working on a new approach to historical research and couldn't get away. Then he began to look for ways to distract Julia from personal concerns and get her focus back on history.

"Julia," he said. "Remember that discussion we had about time travel. You said it was too bad we couldn't go back in time and speak directly to the great historians of the past."

"No, John, You said it was too bad we couldn't transport some of our great historians forward in time so they could provide future biographers and academics with first hand reports. Historians talking to historians; academics talking to academics."

"Yes. Yes that's what you said; you have an incredible mind Julia. You never forget a thing. And what was my reply."

"You were your usual scornful self, and we had a big fight."

"Actually, Julia," John said, "We could probably send a historian into the future if we wanted. Space science has pretty well worked out suspended animation techniques. Think what that would be like. Instead of reading a bunch of dusty old authors who had read other dusty old authors, a trained historian could address future students directly. But who would volunteer for the job?"

"You and I might. We could make history instead of just pontificating about it," Julia said lightly.

"Good God, Julia. Get serious." Then he looked thoughtful. "That certainly would take care of our legacy," and Professor Wilson walked out of the room smiling to himself. He said nothing more, and several days passed.

One morning Julia found him at his desk staring at a pile of papers. He snapped at Julia when he came in. "Damn it, Julia,"' he said. "You should be doing this."
"Doing what?"

"Writing grant proposals. I can't keep an assistant unless I have more money coming into the department." He sighed and put his head down on the desk. Julia didn't move at first. Was this another of his plays for attention?" Finally she came over to him and rubbed the back of his neck.

"John, you aren't really worried are you? With your reputation you've always been able to get anything you want."

""My reputation," he said biting off each syllable, "isn't enough these days. The university system keeps demanding more and more original work, as if I could make history rather than just study it."

"John," said Julia thoughtfully. "Maybe we ought to look into that suspended animation thing. I've been reading about it, and it really is possible. Maybe we actually could make history."

"I know you, Julia. You don't just 'look into something," he said. "You research your subject with the tenacity of a bloodhound. O.K. Give me what you got."

"First you have to consider cryogenics. This goes back to the 1960s and before. The idea was to freeze people who had a terminal illness and keep them that way until science worked out a cure for whatever ailed them. The first person to be frozen was a Dr. James Bedford back in 1967. Of course, there was one big problem. To freeze a living person was out of the question, so they had to wait to the moment of death."

"Yes, I think I remembered that. Sounds a little like the 'Monkey's Paw' to me. Who'd want a wasted, diseased corpse to come back to life?"

"Well apparently someone did. A man named Evan Cooper founded a group called the Life Extension Society in 1964. A year later another group called the Cryonics Society of New York appeared and was following by similar societies in California and Michigan. By 2013 over 270 people have been had their bodies frozen."

"Have any of them been thawed out?" John asked sarcastically.

"Not exactly. Dr. Bedford's body was taken out of storage a couple of times and examined while submerged in liquid nitrogen or something like that. The last time was 1991."

"And?" John said.

"Let's just say he wasn't in very good shape. But that's beside the point, John. Nobody does this anymore. Suspended animation is something different and is done all the time in hospitals when doctors lower a patient's body temperature to protect the brain. Do you remember the case of Gabby Gifford's? She was shot in the head in 2011, and doctors kept her sedated for several days before they were ready to perform surgery."

"O.K., a couple of days but you're talking about years."

"NASA is working on that. They want to send people into space for extended periods, so they've been experimenting with a kind of human hibernation. They use various drugs to put a person into a coma and then they lower his body temperature. All the vital signs are monitored and the condition of the subject is carefully watched."

"And," said John again.

"For a while they reported their progress. Things were looking good, and then the flow of information stopped. They didn't exactly say it was classified, but you just couldn't get any information. Nothing. Nada. I checked with everyone who might know, and it was the same everywhere."

"Interesting," said John. "This means one of two things. They've lost a lot of their people in what will appear to the public to be a huge waste of money and human lives, or..." and he stopped. Professor Wilson had the same look on his face Julia had seen when he was developing some new theory of everything.

"You think they are already doing it?" said Julia. "You think they have people in suspended animation—have had them for some time—maybe years, and they know they can do it safely and wake them up with no loss to body or cognition."

"Exactly. It's a black project, which means big money, probably with military connections. Julie," he smiled, "you are incredible. Keep going."

Research was Julia's forte. She could spend endless, exhaustive hours in the stacks or on the computer searching for the smallest pieces of information and more time putting together pieces of a puzzle. Finally she came to John's office in defeat.

"John, I know it's there. It's a government operation. I'm sure of it," she said slamming a stack of papers down on his desk. "I know it," she said gritting her teeth, "but I run into a blank wall every time I get close. Just when I'm about to find what I want, the information is classified.

"John, it's up to you," she continued. "You have connections higher up. We've met them at those international conferences. Remember that stuffy British Admiral in Luxemburg or that NASA scientist who was so impressed with your speech in Chicago? Let them know you're interested and could suggest an appropriate volunteer."

"And who would that be, Julia, my dear?"

Julia turned on her heels and stalked out the door slamming it behind her.

Suddenly things did open up for Julia. She found a NASA website embedded in an article she was sure she had already checked. She opened it up and stored the information on a flash drive. Then when she went back to look at it again, it was gone. Bingo! John had pulled some strings. He knew how she worked, how she checked and rechecked her notes. He'd charmed someone or twisted a neck or two, and voila, the website was up at a time he knew she'd be in the lab.

The next day Julia stormed into John's office, and slammed some papers down on his desk. "There it is. They're doing it!" The excitement in her voice made John squirm. It was like watching a dog on point. "They need us John. We'll leave a legacy like no other couple in history."

81

"Stop it Julia. You're out of your mind. I'm not going any farther with this, and neither are you." Once again, Julia stalked out slamming the door behind her. Putting his hands behind his head, John let his chair roll back and smiled cautiously. When he left the building that evening he was humming to himself:

Why do the kids put beans in their ears?
Kids cannot hear with beans in their ears.

Less than a week later he had a visitor. "A Major James Clarkson from NASA here to see you, Professor Wilson," the voice on the intercom said.

John and Julia were having another fight. "You called NASA without telling me!" John shouted.

"I did not," Julia proclaimed just as righteously. "I couldn't have gotten through to those people like that. I don't have the clout. It was you. You want this just as much as I do."

"I don't, and I don't want you to do it either."

"Well, it has to be both of us, John. It's your name they want on the project. They already said as much. Think about it. We'll be together. You'll be famous. We'll see the future and will be able to name our own price for speaking engagements."

He'll do it, Julia said to herself. I know he will. He'll argue until the last minute; then he'll do it.

Two weeks later John agreed, on his terms of course. He and the officials from NASA huddled in John's office for hours. Julia was furious when she discovered she was shut out of the negotiations. It was her idea. Did he want all the glory for himself? Would he try to leave her behind?

"Good grief, Julia," John said when they were alone. "The NASA people are calling all the shots. They've been doing this in secret all these years, and now they are ready to go public. It's all PR. They want to focus on one recognizable name. You'll go too. I'll see to it. I simply can't function without my beautiful young assistant," he said as he pulled her into an embrace.

Julia was mollified for the moment. Their lives changed little. They'd all signed NASA contracts and had been sworn to secrecy. There was to be no public notice that might delay the project. Meanwhile NASA's medical personal came and went through the back door.

John had not told his wife. Neither John nor Julia seemed bothered by the lapse. They themselves were not supposed to talk about it even with each other except in the presence of NASA officials. It was a matter of security they said. If one word of this venture reached the media, the government would deny the whole thing.

One day Major Clarkston approached Julia. "You, my dear, will have the honor of going first."

"What do you mean, Major Clarkston? I thought it was understood that we were doing this together."

"You are, my dear. As soon as you are safely in hibernation Professor Wilson will join you. We don't have the equipment to prepare and initiated the initial state for more than one person at a time."

Suddenly Julia felt like her insides were turning to stone. In a panic she turned to John. "I can't. I won't. Do not let them, John. Don't do this this to me."

Professor Wilson took her hands in his and looked into her eyes. "Julia. Julia," he said. "Everything is going to be fine. You and I are going to make history. I will be right beside you, and I'll be there when you wake up. I promise."

NASA SPACE LAB
DIVISION OF HUMAN HYBERNATION AND CRYOGENICS
2060

"Open your eyes, Julia."

"I'm not ready."

"O.K. Just listen to my voice. I need you to wake up."

Julia felt a hand on her cheek. She tried to move away, but couldn't. Fingers slid down her arm and touched her palm. "Squeeze my hand if you feel this." Julia complied.

"Good. Good girl. Now tell me your name."

"Julia Madison."

"Good girl. Can you tell me anymore?"

"Doctor Julia Madison." There was a note of irritation.

"Very good," the voice said close to her head. Then it seemed to turn and direct the next words to a third party somewhere in the room. "I think she is going to be fine."

The reply was slow and reedy. Julia couldn't make out the words.

"Julia," the first voice continued, "Do you remember any more?"

"I volunteered for this."

"You did, Julia, and you will go down in history because of it."

"History is just one damned thing after another," Julia replied.

And from across the room frail voice came again. "That's my girl," Julia's eyes flew open, and she saw a crumpled figure in a wheelchair. *John?*

"John, what have they done to you?" Then she understood.

"NO-o-o-o!" she screamed.

"Sorry, my dear," the old man said, "but I kept my promise. Together we've made history. We're both famous and rich beyond measure. The doctors have kept me alive as long as they could. I'm well over a hundred, but now I must die. I leave history to you."

THE COCKROACH

The Cockroach is one of my favorite stories. The boiler room where Billy meets a talkative insect was inspired by memories if my own elementary school basement. It was a dark mysterious place, and I'm sure it had cockroaches. The rest of the story comes from observing teachers, mothers and their kids, and the way our imagination can run away with the best of us.

"O.K. So I'm a cockroach. Deal with it! "

Billy had been hiding in the school basement since 8:00 am when his dad dropped him off on the way to work.

"Have a great first day of fourth grade, Son," his Dad had said, and that was that. They had driven the entire three-mile trip to school, his Dad with his hands clenched on the steering wheel, the radio turned to a news station, and Billy staring out the window fighting down tears. He was too big to cry.

Billy entered the school, turned left, away from the stream of students funneling into the classrooms, and took the steps that led to the boiler room. No one noticed. He had been hiding in a dirty, bug-infested corner of a storage area ever since. Billy hated bugs. He especially hated cockroaches, and the basement was full of them. Billy had been staring at a particularly large specimen on the wall above his head for the last ten minutes as he tried to get up nerve enough to throw his shoe at it.

Billy was so miserable, the fact that he had actually heard the cockroach speak to him didn't register at first. He'd imagined conversations with animals or inanimate object since he was a toddler, but he was going on ten now and knew the difference between something he made up and something real.

"You're gross," Billy said. "Get lost."

"What do you mean, get lost? You get lost," the cockroach replied. "You're in my space, dude," and it moved a little closer waving its long antennae at him. Billy remembered that cockroaches can fly. He was about to bolt when the janitor galumphed down the stairs and scuffled toward the packing cases where Billy was hiding. Billy put his head down between his knees, made himself small, and held his breath. Mr. Kominski picked up a bucket and mop and left.

"Hey," said the cockroach. "I know why I stay out of that guy's way, but why you? If he sees me, all us down here are in trouble. Out comes the spray gun, the roach traps, the dusts. It's awful, dude, and my missus has her egg cases stored behind these here packing cases. You done something wrong, you go hide someplace else."

A couple of seconds ago Billy was ready to run. Now he was frozen to the spot. He stared at the creature on the wall above him. It was over an inch and a half long with a shiny red-brown body and six hairy legs. Yep, an American Cockroach, a big old Palmetto Bug, and it had just spoken to him.

"I...I...I'm..." Billy sputtered.

"Spit it out, dude," said the cockroach. "Why are you hiding down here? You're supposed to be upstairs in one of them class rooms." The cockroach moved a little closer. Billy shuddered.

"I...I can't go to school right now," he said.

"Why? Don't you like school?" asked the bug waving its antennae.

"Y-yes," Billy sniffed, "but I can't go right now. I need to be home. My mom and dad, they." His voice trailed off. He couldn't say it, couldn't say "divorce." Actually, he didn't know what he would do if he were at home. He just knew he couldn't go to school.

Maybe if he didn't show up in the classroom when all the other kids were getting their desk assignments and signing out their books, there wouldn't be any space left for him, and he wouldn't have to go to school this year. At least not till things straightened out at home.

"You got problems at home?" the bug asked.

Great, thought Billy. Not only could the disgusting creature talk, it could read his mind as well.

***

When Chris McGovern dropped Billy off at Ranger Elementary that morning, he was in a funk over the fight he'd with his wife at breakfast. It happened all to often these days. He'd snap at her about something insignificant. This morning it was the pile of Billy's junk in the hall. He was mad at Billy for being sloppy, mad at his wife for not being a better disciplinarian, mad because the house was too small, when it was his own problems at work that were bothering him.

He felt rotten. His boss was making his life miserable, and he was taking it out on his family. Mary knew something was wrong, but he wasn't the kind to share problems at work with his wife. After all, it was a man's job to protect women from things like that. Mary was such a sweet patient person, but today she had snapped back at him saying she couldn't take his bad moods any more. She would just leave him and take Billy with her.

Instead of apologizing for his behavior, which was what he really wanted to do, he went on the defensive and shouted, "You're not taking my son anywhere," only to see poor Billy standing at the foot of the stairs looking vulnerable and too stunned to cry. Breakfast was served in silence. Nobody ate.

When the clock said 7:45, Chris bundled Billy into the car and headed toward school. He dropped the boy off just before 8:00 and found himself in stop-and-go traffic wondering what to do, go back home and tell Mary he was sorry, or go to work and tell his supervisor to go to hell. Instead of doing either he just continued to drive.

He passed his office building, passed the center of town, passed the car dealers and discount stores out on the highway and continued until he came to a corner diner with a neon sign that blinked "HOT COFFEE – BISCUITS - HOT COFFEE – BISCUITS." Chris suddenly realized he was famished.

***

It was now almost 9, and Valerie Benson's fourth grade room was finally beginning to settle down. Valerie had taken attendance when the late bell rang at 8:10, but she knew by experience that several students would be added

89

or dropped from the roll before the day was over. She and her teaching assistant, Nancy, were seated at Valerie's desk going over the class assignment sheet.

"These children: Here, here, and here." Valerie pointed to three names marked absent. "They're Latino kids. Their parents are probably illegals and have been frightened off by all the nastiness that's going around these days. There's no reason why the children should suffer. We need to find them and get them back in school."

"So that means we keep them on the rolls?" Nancy whispered.

"Definitely, or at least until we know what has happened to them. Now, here." Valerie's finger slid down the sheet. These two will have to be in different class-rooms. They're brothers. It's the rules. Siblings must be separated."

"Good grief. No wonder the office got mixed up," Nancy giggled softly. "Identical twins. Dale Jones and Gale Jones. The office thought they were one person."

"And they're boys," Valerie continued shaking her head. "Why do I think their parents have identity issues? Well, toss a coin, and send one of them to Ms. William's class." Her finger continued on down the list. "I wish I could do the same with this one." She pointed to the name of a girl who was sitting quietly by the window.

"Why? What do you know about her? She seems O.K."
"Oh, it's not her, poor thing. It's her mother. She's convinced the child is too delicate for ordinary activities."

Valerie mimicked the mother's whiny voice. "It's too cold for Susie to play outside today. Susie mustn't sit next to anybody with a runny nose. Susie's too tired for a full day of school today."

"Is there anything really wrong with the child?'

"Well, she has asthma. But so do several other kids at school. It doesn't have to be such a big deal, but ev-er-y thing is a big deal with that woman. Last year she saw a roach in the hall, and the whole school had to be fumigated."

"What about these children?" Nancy pointed to four more names.

"I don't know anything about Betty Jo Kelly or Ricky Weston. Neither of their parents came in for a conference. Rebecca Allen's mother has already called in to say she is sick, but I don't know why Billy McGovern isn't here. Mrs. McGovern had her consultation with me just last week and said Billy was looking forward to fourth grade."

"Should I have the office call?" Nancy asked.

"Maybe you better." Valerie was still looking at the class roll as Nancy left. She glanced up at Susie and sighed thinking, "That child's mother will be in here just about every other day, and God help us if Mrs. Munson sees a cockroach."

***

Down in the boiler room, Mr. Kominsky had returned and slumped into a discarded office chair. It wasn't even noon, and he was already tired. The chair had a broken roller and was lopsided, but the seat and arm rests were padded which made it one of the more comfortable spots in the room. He

91

had pushed it up against a pile of packing cases, the very same packing cases that hid Bill McGovern.

Billy had fallen into a fitful sleep. Neither one was aware of the other. Mr. Kominsky himself was only half awake. This was his normal state these days. It hadn't always been this way, not when Sara was alive. Mr. Kominsky had a tendency to look on the gloomy side of life, but his wife had always had a sunny disposition. She kept him from letting his dark thoughts run away with him. A little joke, a funny story she had heard at the grocery store, a snippet of gossip about this or that had been his reward when he came home from work, but now she was gone.

Mr. Kominsky was depressed, but he would never admit it. He blamed his fatigue on old age. He was, in fact, nearing retirement age, but he had always been healthy, and when he'd had his yearly check-up, the doctor had pronounced him "in good shape for a man of your age." The doctor had failed to ask him any personal questions, and Mr. Kominsky didn't tell him that his wife had died recently.

Mr. Kominsky didn't care much for the doctor anyway. He was too young, too condescending, so he didn't tell the doctor he had trouble sleeping at night and worse trouble staying awake during the day. He didn't tell him he was beginning to hate the job he had always loved.

Maybe he was getting old, but he had two years to go before he could collect his pension. His savings were gone, used up during his wife's illness. He'd mortgaged his house, and now there were no options. He couldn't afford to quit or get fired.
"Gall darn it," he thought. "I'm just going to have to stay out of people's way. If they don't see me, they won't think up things for me to do." Just then a large cockroach scuttled

92

down a near-by packing case, stopped right at eye-level, and waved its antennae at him. Mr. Kominsky got the distinct impression the insect was trying to talk to him.

"Now I know I'm old for this job," he thought. "I'm getting senile."

***

Valerie was becoming irritated. Nancy trotted off to the office to report Billy's absence over 20 minutes ago. She'd been gone far too long for such a simple errand. "Darn," she sighed. "I hope this girl isn't another goof-off."

Last year Valerie's assistant had been more trouble than she was worth, always finding one excuse or another to be out of the classroom, and now it looked like Nancy was going to do the same thing. Valerie fidgeted with her pencil and decided to begin her lecture on homework assignments.

"All right, class. Please put your books away and clear your desk of everything except your pencil and a sheet of notebook paper. We're going to talk about homework. I don't give a lot, but I expect it to be turned in on time. This is very important because you are in fourth grade now, and you will be graded on these assignments. And," she added, "Neatness will count.

Valerie was in the middle of her lecture when Nancy burst into the room nearly tripping over a boy in the back row and began to talk before she had even reached the front of the classroom.
Not now, Nancy," Valerie said sharply. "Whatever it is, it can wait."

"But Ms.. Benson..."

93

"I said not NOW." Valerie practically shouted. Suddenly she was more than irritated. She was furious. A good teacher didn't have to raise her voice in class, and here she was yelling at her assistant on the very first day. Nancy was frightened into silence, but she looked as if she had swallowed a mouth full of hot peppers.

Valerie finished quickly and turned on Nancy glaring. "Never interrupt me in the middle of a lesson, Nancy. Now, what took you so long?"

Nancy took a deep breath and began. "I had the office call Billy McGovern's mother just like you said. Well..." Nancy was warming to her subject. "Well..." she began again. "First they couldn't reach her at home. Then they tried her work number. You know, she wrote down that she worked part time at that flower shop on Main Street, but she wasn't there either so the office called her cell-phone." Nancy was talking so fast she was out of breath.

"Nancy, just calm down and get to the point. Tell me what happened," Valerie said, "but lower your voice.

"Well they finally got her, but she said that Mr. McGovern had taken Billy to school. So the office called Mr. McGovern's business, but he wasn't there either. Then they called Mrs. McGovern back and told her. Well...at first Mrs. McGovern got—like, you know—real quiet, and then she began yelling. I could hear from the other side of the room." Nancy's voice began to rise.

"She was saying, 'You find my husband. He has Billy. You find my child or I'll call the police.' That's what she said, Ms. Benson. She said she was going to call the police."

"Nancy, will you please keep your voice down," Valerie hissed, but Nancy was too excited to stop. "Ms. Benson, Mrs. McGovern thinks her husband kidnapped Billy. She's calling the police."

The word "kidnapped" echoed from one end of the classroom to the other. When Valerie looked around, every child in the room was staring at her. Just then, off in the distance they could all hear the wail of a police siren.

***

Officer Richards arrived at Ranger Elementary just as Susie Munson's mother was pulling into the parking lot with Susie's inhaler. In the excitement of the first day of school, Susie had left it behind on the kitchen table. When Mrs. Munson saw the police car pull up to the entrance of the school and Office Richards enter the building at what appeared to be a run, she clutched at the steering wheel and hit the accelerator instead of the break.

There was a sickening crunch of metal as her Jeep Cherokee rammed into a large blue minivan. Mrs. Munson promptly burst into tears. She knew there was only one thing to do now. When one has an accident, one reports it to the police. Always prepared for the worst, Mrs. Munson had the number already programmed into her cell-phone.

"I want to report an accident at Ranger Elementary School," she informed the dispatcher at the police station. The dispatcher tried to get some more information, but a distraught Mrs. Munson was no longer listening. "I'm going inside to find my child," she sobbed and snapped the cell-phone shut.

***

Billy's mom had been pulling into the West End Shopping Mall parking lot when the when the school reached her the second time to say that neither, Billy, or her husband could be found. Mrs. McGovern promptly turned the car around and headed back into traffic. She had driven through her second stop sign without slowing down when she was spotted by a patrol car.

Officer Johnston motioned to her to pull over. When she ignored him, the officer hit the siren and took off after her. Mrs. McGovern was nearing the school just as Mrs. Munson jumped out of her car and ran sobbing toward the building. It was Officer Johnston's siren the children heard as Nancy blurted out her announcement of a possible kidnapping.

Up in Valerie's Benson's fourth grade class-room all sense of order and discipline was beginning to crumble. Nancy stood in the front of the room looking bug-eyed and wringing her hands. The children were out of their seats and rushing toward the windows. Valerie turned on her assistant.

"Get out. Get out of my class right now. Go to the office, and stay there until I send for you." Nancy looked stunned but did as she was told. Valerie walked to the windows with the intention of calmly directing her students back to their seats, but when she looked down into the parking lot she too began to lose her composure.

Below her she could see one police car parked by the door. Another was pulling up to what appeared to be an accident, and a third could be seen tearing down the street toward the school, its blue lights flashing and its siren rising and falling like the opening of a TV cop show. Mrs. McGovern and Office Johnston reached the front of the building at the same time.

It was the beginning of a perfect storm.

***

On the third floor of the apartment building across the street from Ranger Elementary, Edna Lakoff was on the phone talking to her sister who lived across town. Edna's daughter was getting married next month, and Edna found a reason to consult her sister every day.

"I found the perfect dress, Betty. Just perfect, and I got shoes to match. Well, the dress is a little tight... but, oh! It's so-o-o just right for the occasion, and I know I can lose a few pounds before the wedding."

"I'm not so sure, Edna. You know how much trouble you have sticking to a diet, and you'll be under a lot of tension the next few weeks. You always eat when you're nervous. Maybe you had better keep looking."

"How can you say that, Betty? I can lose weight when I want to. I'll just go on that grapefruit diet for a few days." Suddenly Edna gasped. "Oh! Oh, my God."

"Edna, what's the matter?" Silence. "Edna, answer me."

"Betty, something has happened at the school."

"What do you mean?" What happened? How do you know?"

"Betty, our apartment is on the second story. I can see the school out the window. There are police cars all over the

97

place. Goodness, I hope there hasn't been one of those awful shootings. I'm going down and see," and Edna hung up.

Betty tried to call her back. When she couldn't reach her, she called a friend who lived just a block down from the school and had a child in the third grade. "Rita, something happened at Ranger Elementary. There are police all around the school. Edna thinks maybe there has been a shooting." There was a gasp at the other end of the line, and Rita hung up.

Rita called her husband at work in the business section of town. "Frank, there's been a shooting at Johnny's school. Get over there right away." Frank hung up, grabbed his car keys, and bolted for the door.

Looking back later, no one could say for sure who called the local T.V. station.

***

In the basement of Ranger Elementary, Billy and Mr. Kominsky were startled into wakefulness at the same instant. The wail of the police siren was muted but still had the ability to inject a certain feeling of urgency into any situation. Mr. Kominsky lost his balance on the broken chair and slid to the floor; Bill couldn't remember where he was and knocked over one of the packing cases. The cockroach that had been watching them from the ceiling took sanctuary in a dark corner of the room.
Outside, the third patrol car shut off its Siren, and in the stillness that followed Mr. Kominsky and Billy stared at each other. A befuddled Billy who had been dreaming about giant insects said the first thing that came to his head. "There are cockroaches down here."

"No. No they ain't." Mr. Kominsky knew trouble when he saw it. A kid hiding in his storage space was bad enough, but the little bugger was about to tell the world the place was infested. He'd lose his job for sure.

"No way. Not here. You were dreaming," he said with as much conviction as he could muster. He'd better get the kid out of here before the boy saw any more incriminating evidence.

Mr. Kominsky thought he heard laughter coming from high up in the corner of the room.

Billy rubbed his eyes and began to sneeze. The dust had gotten up his nose and was irritating his already tear-reddened eyes. Now he began to cry in earnest. "My mom and dad are going to get a divorce," he blubbered.

Mr. Kominsky was far from a heartless man, but it had been a long time since he tried to comfort a frightened and unhappy child. He struggled to get up. "Crying won't help," he said," and maybe you're wrong. Maybe you just think they going to get a divorce."

"They are. I heard them. They had a big fight this morning, and Mom said she was leaving and taking me with her. Dad yelled at her and said, 'No way. You're not taking my son anywhere.' They were fighting over me. Now they're going to get a divorce, and it's my fault."

"No, it's not. No way," said Mr. Kominsky, and he reached out to touch the child; but Billy pulled away. "Come on," Mr. Kominsky said gently. "You can't stay down here."

"I'm not leaving." Billy was adamant.

Mr. Kominsky knew he had better get upstairs before someone came down to find him. It was best to keep people out of his domain for the time being. "Come on," he tried again. "We're going to get you cleaned up."

"No, I'm not leaving. You can't make me." Billy pressed himself further back behind the packing cases. "Suit yourself," replied the janitor. He brushed the dust off his uniform and headed for the stairs.

Billy sniffled a bit and put his head down. The room was quiet now. Slowly the cockroach came out of hiding and began to creep down the wall. When he was on a level with Billy's head, he waved his antennae.

"Stop it!" he demanded. "You stop feeling sorry for yourself." Billy looked up. The cockroach was inches away from his face. This time Billy was too exhausted to react. He simply rubbed his eyes with the back of his hand and sniffled. "Why should I?"

"Cause you don't know nothing about trouble," replied the cockroach. "You try being a cockroach. Everybody hates cockroaches. It's always open season on us. I saw you. You were going to throw your shoe at me a while ago."

"Well, you are pretty ugly, and you give people asthma. Susie's mom say so," replied Billy, but he was feeling a little sorry for the insect now. It was hard to talk to something and not feel a certain empathy with it. Billy never let his mom throw out his old stuffed animals, not even when they'd grown ragged and he was too old to play with them anymore. They'd been real once.

The cockroach was incensed. "Wait a minute. You just wait a cotton-pickin' minute. Who are you calling ugly? Look at you, all pasty white. No antennae, no hair on your arms... and you only got two of them anyway."

"Sorry," said Billy, and he looked so miserable it was the cockroach's turn to be sympathetic.

"Suppose you tell me why you can't go upstairs with everybody else. I'll listen. Ain't got nothin' else to do anyway."

***

It was now after 10 and Chris McGovern had been drinking coffee and staring at a TV mounted in the corner of the room for almost two hours. Suddenly an announcer broke in. "We have some breaking local news. There has been some sort of incident at Ranger Elementary School. Police have surrounded the building and nobody is being allowed in or out. Our mobile camera team has just arrived on the scene. Tell us what is going on Veronica."

Chris stood up spilling the dregs from his third cup of regular down the front of his trousers. On the screen an attractive, well-coiffed newswoman was holding a microphone. In the background he could see the front door at Ranger Elementary, the same door that Billy had entered less than three hours ago.

"Turn the sound up," Chris yelled at the man behind the counter. He moved closer and heard the woman talking to someone off camera.
"Excuse me Sir. Can you tell me your name?"

"I'm Frank Cranston. I have a boy in third grade. Please get out of my way. I need to find out what happened." The man pushed past the woman and ran up the steps. No one stopped him. The woman turned to another individual.

"Excuse me, Madam. Can you tell me your name?" This person seemed eager to talk. She was patting her hair and smiling at the cameraman.

"I'm Edna Thomas, and I live in that apartment building right over there. See that window on the second floor? Well, I was right there on the phone talking to my sister. My daughter's getting married next month, you know, and I could see the police cars arriving. I figured there'd been a shooting or something."

Chris didn't wait to hear any more. He grabbed a bill from his wallet, slapped it on the counter, and bolted out to the car. It took him 20 minutes to reach Ranger Elementary. The police cars were still there. So was the TV truck, but newswoman was nowhere to be seen, and when Chris parked and ran up the steps to the door, nobody stopped him either. Inside the building he headed for the principal's office. The door was open and through it he saw his wife talking to an elderly man in a janitor's uniform.

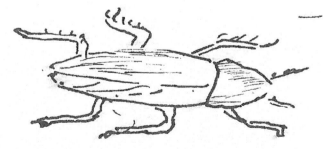

Down in the basement Bill had stopped crying. He had gotten use to talking to the cockroach by now and was unburdening himself.

"So you think your mom and dad are going to get a divorce because they had a fight?" the insect asked.

Billy nodded.

"You got a best friend?"

"Yah, Ricky. He lives across the street from me."

"You two ever fight?

"Sure, but that's different. We're guys. We like to fight sometime."

"Okay, well... parents don't exactly like to fight, but they do it sometimes. Then they make up. I bet your parents have made up already."

"You think so?"

"Don't know," said the cockroach, "but the only way you'll find out is to go upstairs and tell someone to call them."

And get the dickens out of my space, he thought to himself, before someone comes down here and begins to look around.

Billy was feeling much better. He'd had about enough of the dark stuffy basement anyway. He was ready to do whatever the cockroach suggested.

"Just one thing before you go," said the insect. Don't say anything about cockroaches. Old man Kominski will lose his job, and me and the Missus will be out of a home. Mr. Kaminski's a lonely old man, Billy. If you really want to do something good, be his friend. He needs someone to talk to. Cockroaches know these things."

Billy mounted the stairs and started down the hall toward the door he had entered a few hours ago. Then he heard his parent's voices coming from the principal's office. They were both talking at once, but they didn't sound like they were fighting any more. He looked in through the partly open door and saw them with Mr. Kominski. Maybe the cockroach was right. They had made up, and they weren't going to get a divorce after all.

As he watched, he saw his dad pull his mom close. She was holding him around the waist like she did in their wedding photos. They sure didn't look like they were going to get a divorce.

"Billy's down in the basement," Mr. Kominski was telling them. "He's fine, but don't you go down there. He says he wants to come up here by himself, him being a fourth grader and all. He's sorry he scared you, but just remember, he's a little emotional right now so don't take anything he says too seriously. I'll just go tell him you're here."

Mr. Kominski turned toward the door, but he didn't have to go anywhere. Billy burst though it and ran to his parents' open arms. Nope, Billy thought. They certainly weren't going to get a divorce. Things were going to be just fine, and he and Mr. Kominski were going to be good friends. He might even become friends with the cockroach. Yes, Bill was going to have a great first day in fourth grade.

Mr. Kaminsky

Essays

Over the years I have written a great many letters, columns, and other pieces, some of which are gathered here under the heading, "Essays. They reflect my interest in science and contemporary culture.

Most have them have been published on the opinion page of Gainesville Times and other media out lets. Newspapers are always happy when readers write back, and this leads me to another concern. Communication itself.

No matter how hard I tried to be polite and even handed, I was sure to make someone mad. Mankind is misnamed. Homo Sapiens is not a logical animal at all, nor is he wise. Humankind is driven by emotion, and thus the race is in jeopardy. However, as a writer I must pay homage to this unique quality. It is the source of all literature.

The Panama Canal

SYNCHRONICITY

I have a note taped up over my computer that reads: "Be prepared for synchronicity in your life. It grew out of some unnamed force somewhere in the universe. Acknowledge it when it appears. Be grateful and give thanks, for if you think deeply you will find it is not random at all."

According to Merriam and Webster, synchronicity is the coincidental occurrence of events that seem related but cannot be explained by conventional mechanisms of causality. Developed by Carl Jung in the 1920s, synchronicity postulates relationships that are not governed by cause and effect, but are nonetheless meaningful, at least to the individual who experiences them.

Most of the important occurrences in my life were synchronistic. That is, they appeared to be accidental. The dictionary definition of accidental does include "random," but the reverse isn't true. Random is something else, and therein lies a question. Is there another system or structure at work in the cosmos?

Einstein said, "God does not play dice with the universe." This seems to rule out accidents, but not synchronicity. Einstein also posed his own question, "Is the universe a friendly place?" Apparently he wasn't sure. He said it depends on how the world uses its resources—its scientific discoveries and its technology. Misused, they will most assuredly destroy us.

If the universe is neither friendly nor unfriendly, our fate depends on chance, on a toss of the cosmic dice—a thing that Einstein apparently rejected. However he said, "If we decide that the universe is a friendly place, we will use our technology, our scientific discoveries and our natural resources to create tools and models for understanding that universe."

This leaves us with two different futures for mankind, and this is where synchronicity enters the picture. One can bring God into the equation if they like, but both Einstein and Jung were scientists. They were not believers. They were thinkers. They questioned. They searched for patterns and order. They developed hypotheses. They constructed theories that would be tested. When they did speak, it was out of something deeper than belief.

Physical change through time is universal, but it is not random. It follows certain natural laws. If cause and effect are the only factors involved, if nothing is random, if everything is pre-determined, then there is no free will. (Let me warn the reader, there is a very good case for this.)

If there is no free will, if we can't change the path we are on today, the human race is in trouble because the forces at work in society today are controlled by money, ego, and the drive for power.

If there is another system at work, one based on relationships and meaning, perhaps we *will* use our technology, our scientific discoveries, and our natural resources; to change the path humanity is on now. It doesn't matter if you believe in a personal God or an evolving human spirit. It matters how you act. And how you act depends largely on how you think.

Is the Earth here for you to exploit, or is it here for you to protect and nurture? Do you stand; alone against the forces of nature, or are you part of a vast network of sentient creatures?

I'm not sure what role synchronicity plays in our lives, but I do know it depends upon individuals who are open to it when it happens.

I would like to believe we can change the path we are on.

I want to believe the universe is a friendly place.

ABOUT WAR

I'll start with a quote my brother found in a book he was
reading, *The Sense of an Ending* by Julian Barnes.
Although it doesn't directly pertain to warfare, it has a lot
to say about the history of war. "History, that certainty
produced at the point where the imperfections of memory
meet the inadequacies of documentation." Think about it.

It struck me as particularly insightful, and I sent it on to an
old friend from college. She responded with a quote of her
own, and our exchange continued. Since she is more widely
traveled than I am, her quotes became rather far-reaching
and exotic. For instance, "In every kitchen, they're cooking
beans."

Apparently, this is an old Spanish proverb. She had to
explain it to me. It has something to do with being
suspicious. I still don't get it, but one quote she didn't have
to explain came from *Let The Great World Spin* by Colum
McCann: "The only thing you need to know about war,
son, is: Don't go.

My apologies to the loyal men and women who volunteer
to serve our country, but my Quaker instincts tell me
McCann is right. "Don't go!" Violence begets violence.
Especially today when even the threat of armed conflict
could trigger a nuclear exchange.

A more universal perspective comes from one of the key
figures in the development of the atomic bomb, Albert
Einstein. He spoke the following lines on national
television just after President Truman announced that the
United States would begin work on a H-bomb. "Every

step," he said, "appears as the unavoidable consequences of the preceding one. In the end, there beckons more and more clearly general annihilation."

This particular quote appears in *Command and Control,* an exceptionally well-documented history of nuclear weapons. Not the kind of book I enjoy reading read right now, but it's my job as a board member of Nuclear Watch South to keep up with these things.

No one knows for sure how many nuclear bombs there are in the world today. Their exact number and location are closely guarded secrets of the nine nations that possess them, but various organizations track this kind of information and agree that there are probably over seventeen thousand, many of them on high-alert status and ready to fire. This means with the passage of time, an accidental launch is almost certain.

I'm sure *Times* readers understand what a single modern thermonuclear bomb could do. We know, but we block it out, and thus, as Einstein said over 50 years ago, the human race drifts toward annihilation.

I could tell horror stories about accidents and near launches, about the poor conditions and poor morale of the men in our underground missile-launch bunkers, about the brinksmanship that occurs at the highest level of governments around the world, but it would be counterproductive. Fear and resignation are our worst enemies. On the other hand, denial is not an option.

Our task now—as individuals and as human beings—is to come up with ways to change the course we are on. And yes, that means a certain amount of radical change. When

Pope Francis said, "Unfettered capitalism is a form of tyranny." He was accused of being a Marxist, but the Pope wasn't suggesting we become Marxists, only that we need to redirect our economic system away from greater and greater corporate profit and toward worldwide social needs.

If humanitarian concerns don't move you, consider the cost. According to Reuters News Service, the U.S. plans to spend approximately $355 billion dollars modernizing our nuclear arsenal in the next ten years. Furthermore, the cost is not just dollars and cents. Living under the threat of nuclear annihilation is demoralizing.

Last quote: "Every weapon that is made is a theft from those who hunger and are not fed, those who are cold and not clothed. A world in arms is not spending money alone. It is spending the sweat of its laborers, the genius of its scientists, the hopes of it children ... it is humanity hanging from a cross of iron." Dwight Eisenhower.

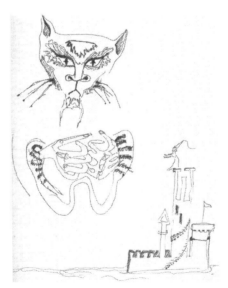

Give Me Guns!

USE YOUR BRAIN

No doubt you've heard this before. You've probably said it to someone yourself. (Most likely to one of your kids.)

Use your brain, but which part of the brain? Once, this question wouldn't have made much sense. Now, using magnetic resonance imaging (MRI), neuroscientists can watch as different parts of the brain turn on and off as it processes incoming messages.

We can actually see the brain receive a stimulus and form a response, and when the brain takes in information contrary to its owner's preconditioning—his or her cultural, religious, or political beliefs—the brain registers discomfort and begins to rationalize the information away. It bypasses the area of the brain that deals in facts and moves to a part of the circuitry that make its owner feel better.

According to Professor Drew Westen of Emory University, it the same part of the brain that makes drug addicts feel good about getting high. In other words, stress reduction takes precedent over rational thinking.

Consider the amount of stress in everyday life today: the economy, global climate change, technology run amuck, gonzo politics, and round-the-clock news coverage that never lets you take an easy breath. It's easy to see why there's a lot of irrational thinking going on.

Fear can sharpen the senses, but it doesn't always enhance our problem solving abilities, and those who seek power are not above using our fears and anxieties to their own ends. Think about this next time you hear a political

114

speech. How many times does a politician promise to be tough on crime or illegal immigrants? How often do media pundits prey on our insecurities rather than appeal to our better nature?

Humans are primates, and the great apes are our nearest relatives in the animal kingdom. Anyone who studies them knows that sex and power (the struggle for status within the group) are behind almost everything they do. But where chimps and other great apes are openly sexual, mankind hides behind cloth and closed doors. Where humans strive for power, they hide their motive behind high-sounding words. Essentially, primates share the same drives.

Those who long for power and prestige—and to some extent this is all of us—don't talk about it directly. They talk about service and "giving something back." Nevertheless, power itself is no more a bad thing than sex is. Orderly human interaction requires a hierarchy of some sort. It requires laws. It requires government. We don't need to guard against government as much as we need to guard against those—in government or out—who manipulate our weaknesses to advance their own agenda.

Observing our primate cousins can teach us something else: Altruism is as much a genetic trait as the lust for power or sex. It had its beginnings when mammals began to nurse their young. Any primatologist who has spent time watching the higher apes can recount numerous selfless acts not only within the group but across species as well.

Frans De Waal, in his book *Our Inner Ape*, describes watching a bonobo (relative of the chimpanzee) pick up an injured bird, climb a tree, and gently spread the bird's wings in an attempt to get it to fly. When it fluttered to the ground, she descended and stood guard over the injured animal until it recovered and flew off.

115

There have been enough studies about violence and not enough about harmonious living. Listen carefully next time you hear a voice designed to stir your passions. If it is divisive, if it preys on your anxieties, turn it off. Use your brain, but use it to solve problems not appease your prejudices.

TECHNOLOGY

My father was an electrical engineer. He considered himself a scientist. Born November 4, 1899 he was a life-long employee of the Bell Laboratories. On more than one occasion he told me, "If I live to be a hundred, my life will span three centuries."

He didn't make it, but he lived long enough to experience two world wars and the dawn of the Nuclear Age. I was born in 1932. As middle-class Americans we had electricity, indoor plumbing, an automobile, and other comforts of life but nothing even approaching the technical gadgetry common to the average American family today. The technical advances in my lifetime alone are greater than anything humanity has experienced in all its history.

My father liked all thing technical, and to illustrate how fast technology was expanding he would draw a graph. On the bottom-line from left to right he plotted human technology: the first stone tools, the discovery of fire, the wheel, and finally electricity and the industrial revolution. On the vertical arm he indicated the rate at which technology was advancing.

The graph showed a line that was nearly flat for most of human history. An upward curve began in the last few hundred years and then climbed sharply as it reached the present. Most of mankind's technical advances fell within our two lifetimes. Technology was growing geometrically. Dad would point to this and warn that in my lifetime alone the line would begin a near vertical ascent. "What will happen to human society at that point," my father said, "will be beyond imagination."

To a child, this view of the future was disturbing. Even in my teens I sensed we were in trouble. Technology was advancing at a staggering rate, but human nature had changed very little over the last hundred thousand years.

Engineering was the first science. Physics and chemistry evolved from astrology and alchemy. Then came the social sciences. Psychology emerged as a separate discipline less than 150 years ago. Only in the last few years have we begun to study the human brain. Today we can watch as a subject deals with his emotions. However, this kind of neuroscience is in its infancy, and of human consciousness we know next to nothing. "I think, there for I am," is about as far as it goes.

So here's our dilemma. Technology has given us wonderful things: the ability to replace organs and prolong life. We have invaded space. We have gone to the depth of the sea. We can travel around the world in hours; communicate around the globe in seconds. We can manipulate DNA ... the very basis of life itself.

On the other hand, mankind has never been more vulnerable. A single nuclear exchange could destroy thousands of years of civilization, and environmental pollution is even now fouling the oceans, the soil, and the air we breathe. Subconsciously, we're all aware of the threat, and a strange sort of depression is settling over humanity.

It's reflected in our music, our movies, and in the economy. We will not willingly give up our technical magic. Money and power cannot be beaten on their own ground. We cannot destroy the things that threaten us. We can only transcend them.

We are in a second Dark Age, only this time it is psychological. According to a report in the Wall Street Journal, one in five Americans are taking some form of mood-altering drug. If technology is making life better, why do we do this? Something is missing. Until we figure this out, we're on the road to self-annihilation.

The obvious answer is a spiritual reawakening, but that's not going to come from religion as it's practiced today. No one faith has all the answers, but our competitive nature causes religions to fight among ourselves rather than work together.

"When we will ever learn. When will we ever learn?"
(Pete Seeger)

SCIENCE FICTION

Scientific fact provides a scaffolding for the future, but science fiction provides the imagination that makes the future possible. Science fiction writers of the 20th century are the prophets of today. They laid the groundwork for the space age.

Science fiction is a bit like scripture. Scripture plumbs the depth of the human psyche and brings it to life in the form of metaphor and myth. The Old Testimony prophets saw into the future, made their predictions, and issued their warnings. Today's science fiction writers, the good ones anyway, do the same thing.

I just finished rereading Aldous Huxley's *Brave New World*. It was published the year I was born and reaches deep into the future. I read *1984* when I was in college. Both are futuristic novels with very similar themes, a time when humanity is in grave danger of losing its soul.

In Author C. Clarke's sci-fi novel, *Childhood's End* the human soul is not so much lost as it is transcended, but each of these three science fiction stories asks much the same question: "What happens to humanity when it ceases to struggle for freedom of thought and independent action?" In 1984 this freedom is sapped by pain and ignorance. In *Brave New World* it is crippled by pleasure and soma. In *Childhood's End* Man is dominated by a powerful overload from space.

Today mankind is in trouble. We accept the many miracles of science and never realize that everything comes with a price. We pollute the land and trash the seas, and when we realize the mess we have made, we expect science to save us. It can't.

Science can only provide the tools. It can't heal the psyche. Science fiction operates not on fact but on imagination, which Albert Einstein said is more important than knowledge. "Knowledge is limited. Imagination encircles the world."

I'm not sure just how science fiction can rescue us from ourselves, but the best science fiction is an art form. Like any other art form, it communicates on a higher level than mere reality, and it speaks a higher form of truth.

FOUR OLD CODGERS

The news about the four old codgers who wanted to bomb government buildings and kill a "bucket list" of people—including media personnel—broke on a Tuesday. The story of their arrest was on the front page of the *Gainesville Times* on Wednesday, and by Thursday it was in the *New York Times*.

It just so happened that I spent most of that Thursday in a government building, and as a guest columnist for the Gainesville Times, I suppose I qualify as "media personnel." Suddenly this terrorism business was getting up-close and personal.

I was in court Thursday as a CASA, a court appointed special advocate for children. Here are a few of those who would have been hurt if someone had bombed the building: An adorable three-year-old girl sitting next to me, several sets of grandparents and at least two foster parents, the kind of people who step in to comfort and care for frightened children when the Department of Family and Children's Services (DFACS) is forced to take them into custody, a number of overworked, underpaid advocate coordinators from DFACS, and a handful of CASA volunteers.

And this is just a partial list of the good people who work for positive change though state and federal programs. I wonder if any of those angry men thought about this in their quest to bring down "da gub'ment"?

I don't know what will happen to those four old men ... all younger than me, by the way. Their arrest was some sort of

122

sting operation by the FBI, and the newspapers kept referring to the testimony of "a confidential source, currently on bond for pending felony charges." That certainly gives me pause, but I have run into this type of obfuscation before.

Not too long ago I encountered another "old codger" expounding on politics, government, and the media in our local coffee shop. He was loud, rude, and thoroughly obnoxious. "Yes," he announced making sure everyone around him could hear. "I'm opinionated and proud of it. This country is going to hell, and it's the fault of ..." and he launched into a long list of perceived miscreants in language I can't use in the papers."

Unpleasant but probably harmless, I thought at the time. Now I'm not so sure. I believe in free speech and the right to voice one's opinion as much as the next person. It is the mark of a civilized nation, but a nation where people have no respect for others or for the rule of law is not civilized.

Furthermore, words become weapons when they spread fear and distrust. Our government is not perfect, not by a long shot. We need basic reform at every level, but somebody needs to stand up and defend government on general grounds. The opposite of government is anarchy, and anarchy is an untamed beast.

Today the world is in crisis, but then it always has been. It's just that in the past we didn't have television and the internet to hype every conflict and every injustice. You've heard the old adage: "You are what you eat." A strong, healthy body is not built on junk food and soda pop. In the same vein, a strong, healthy mind is not built on angry words and bombastic rhetoric.

It is not such a big step from blaming the government for every possible problem to justifying bringing the government down with violence. It's been a week now since the four men were arrested, two weeks by the time this column is published. There was nothing more about the men in the paper today, but I'm not ready to let it go.

I don't want vengeance. I do want people to pay attention to what they say in public ... and in private. Hate is a cancer, and it's contagious. Opinions are not benign word play. They can be the vector of the cancer.

COSMIC WAR

Our granddaughter's school requires all eighth grade students to study the Old Testament. The course is called World Religions, but the text comes from the Bible. In high school students study the New Testament.

I believe religion should be part of every child's formal education, but I'm not sure parts of the Old Testament are fit reading for a thirteen-year old. The Old Testament is a bloody, unforgiving chronicle.

For example: First Samuel (15.1) where God commands, "Kill both man and woman, child and infant, ox and sheep, camel and donkey," or Joshua Chapter 10 where, on God's orders, Joshua attacks city after city killing every creature living within. Read about how Jehu demonstrated his "zeal for the Lord" by massacring every inhabitant of Samaria. (Kings 10.15-17) And this is just a small sampling.

When I hear Christians attack Islam because parts of the Qur'an call for Holy War, I wonder—do these people ever read their own scripture? It does seem that at one time or another every religion tells its followers to slay the unbelievers.

Mankind is a bloodthirsty lot ... but killing in the name of God? Surely it is the very worst kind of religious perversion. Nevertheless, it happens over and over again when people see themselves fighting on God's side in a war of good against evil. Earthly life means nothing to them because their battle is not located in time and space. It is fought on a cosmic level.

Reza Aslan in his book *How to Win a Cosmic War* analyzes the phenomena but is sketchy when it comes to explaining why a given individual falls prey to this kind of warped thinking. Apparently it isn't poverty or lack of intelligence. It isn't even a flawed education. It appears to be a lack of personal identity.

By themselves these people are nothing, but by linking themselves to demanding God, they become invincible. Their cause, whatever it is—nationalism, anti-abortion, racial or sexual purity—becomes a crusade, and it doesn't matter if they blow themselves up in a crowded market or go to prison for murdering a doctor. Life means nothing to them.

Human beings are a complicated species. We take our identity from many sources: family, friends, community, nation, and church, but only religion promises immortality through the simple act of believing. When ties to family, friends, community, and nation are weak, the emotional power of religion can become toxic and overwhelm any sense of human goodness or love of God's creation.

A little child takes what it wants and feels justified in whatever it does. Limits come first from the family, then the community, and finally the government. Religion attempts to teach a moral code, but there is no uniformity in belief, not even within the various Christian denominations.

This is why a wall of separation between church and state is so important, and this is why inflammatory statements by politicians, religious spokespersons, and media pundits are so dangerous. They create a rift in the fabric of our nation that weakens us all. Elections, court nominations, and the operation of state and federal offices break down along lines that have nothing to do with national security or effective government.

Oh yes, and people occasionally get killed.

It will be interesting to see what my granddaughter learns in her religion course next year. For my part I have tried to instill in her a respect for all religions and for the majesty and basic goodness of God's creation. There is no one-size-fits-all approach to faith. Each of us has to find it for himself.

How to win a cosmic war? According to the inside flap of the book's dust cover ... by refusing to fight one.

A MODERN FAIRY TALE

See if this plot sounds familiar: The hero is an orphan who runs away from cruel foster parents at an early age. There's a dragon loose in the land that is stealing young virgins in order to possess their beauty. The hero, seeking fame and fortune, joins the King's Guard where he is told he must find the dragon and slay him, but the only one who knows where the dragon sleeps is a powerful magician.

The magician, however, is very dangerous. Once he was a healer, but he has become corrupt and is eating people so the King has him locked away deep in a dungeon. The hero descends into the abyss to see the magician. On the way he passes many horrible creatures that hiss and spit at him but do not frighten him away. He reaches the magician, who also tries to scare him off with his magic powers but does not succeed.

Finally the magician tells the hero he does indeed know where the dragon is, but all he will give the hero is a clue. With the clue the hero finds the dragon's spoor, but that is not enough. Meanwhile the dragon steals the King's daughter. The hero returns and tries to trick the magician into giving him more information.

At first the magician is taken in, but the magician's cruel jailer becomes jealous of the power the youth is gaining over his captive and reports to the King. The angry King has the jailer bring the magician to the palace so he can question him personally. The King, however, learns nothing.

Once again the hero visits the magician. This time he has to do it surreptitiously. The jailer finds out and has the hero thrown out of the palace, but not before the magician has given the youth another clue.

The King is careless and the magician escapes, but the second clue is all the hero needs. He tracks the dragon to his lair where the King's daughter is being kept in a deep well. The hero enters the lair, slays the dragon, and saves the princess. The King rewards the hero, and the dangerous magician leaves the country in pursuit of the wicked jailer whom he plans to eat.

Is this some fairy tale or an ancient fable? No. It's the plot of *The Silence of the Lambs*, a 1991 movie thriller directed by Jonathan Demme and starring Jodie Foster and Anthony Hopkins.

On the surface the *Silence of the Lambs* is a graphic and rather gross horror story, but its success at the box office suggests there is something more to it. If you've read Joseph Campbell, you know that myths and fairy tales are a way mankind deals with the uncertainties of life.

The hero is our self. It is we who must set forth in the world, must pass tests, deal with tricksters, descend into the abyss, and slay dragons, but our myths reassure us: We are the pure, the good, and will eventually win over all odds.

"Just as dreams are messages the subconscious sends to the individual, myths are messages the collective unconscious sends to the group. Our movies, like myths and fairy tales, are a way our culture communicates with itself. Make-believe allows us to express things we would otherwise hide."

We play all the parts, villain as well as hero, and thus we tell ourselves universal truths that we're unable to face in any other form. The Silence of the Lambs was a top moneymaker in 1991. It won Academy Awards in all top five categories, and in 2011 was selected by the U. S. Library of Congress for preservation in the National Film Registry.

In the movie the hero and the authority figure are women. The hero is a young FBI trainee, Clarice Starling. The evil magician is Hannibal Lecter. The King is a female senator and mother of the stolen princess. The dragon is a psychopathic killer who captures young women to obtain their skin.

The hero is of humble birth but is clever and brave as well as good and pure of heart. Thus she assures us of our own worth and intelligence. The magician represents both the spiritual and the demonic. He possesses great power. He can read minds. He can see what others cannot, and he is dangerous for he is likely to devour us.

It is not the hero who chooses to turn to the magician for help, but the government, her superiors in the FBI. The hero, however, is willing because she seeks advancement. Clarice is successful in learning the secret of the dragon's lair from the demon/god figure, but because of error on the part of the authorities, the demon is released into the world, in effect, destroying one danger while setting lose another.

There IS danger in the world today. Horrible, unspeakable things can happen. The movie not only conditions us to the horror, it tells us we will be given the power to overcome. Clarice Starling is warned that Hannibal, the mad psychiatrist, will try to get inside her mind and control her, but she successfully resists him, and she uses his powers to find the killer before the senator's daughter is sacrificed. The dragon is slain but the demon escapes.

The movie ends on a reassuring note when Hannibal phones Clarice to say that she herself has nothing to fear from him since he has another more interesting game to pursue... for now. There are many evils in the real world, and we *are* called upon to slay dragons. We are told we must use whatever power is necessary to do this, even if it means descending into the abyss to bargain with a demonic force.

The movie reassures us that even if this demonic force does escape, it will be someone else's fault, not ours, and we ourselves will not be subject to retribution... for now.

A LESSON FROM MATT

Rocco was known to be a harsh man. He'd grown up on the streets and become rich on ill-gotten gains. Rocco started out running a protection racket. Then he got into prostitution. He was even charged with a murder or two, but nothing stuck because he'd always bullied others into doing the dirty work for him. Now, however, the Feds were after him for income tax evasion, and it looked like he was going to serve time.

He hired a battery of expensive lawyers. "Rocco," one of them said, "you better prepare yourself. Seven to ten years is the best we can get for you. Stash your money somewhere. Keep your nose clean while you're in the can, and maybe we can get you out in five."

Rocco summoned his henchmen, announced he was going on a trip and was entrusting them with his money. To his top man he gave five million dollars. "Blackie," he said, "you're like a son to me. Take care of this while I'm away." Then he called his other two knuckle men. "Joey, you know the ropes. I'm giving you two million. You'll know how to handle it."

Finally he addressed Louie the newest and youngest of his three stooges. "We're going to see how you do. I'm going to give you a million. Take good care of it, and there will be an important place for you in the organization when I get out." The next day he turned himself in at the Federal Pen.

Blackie picked up where his boss left off. He ran the rackets and avoided the police. In the next few years he doubled the money his boss had left him. Joey took his money, moved to a different city and began building his own network of shady operations. Louie, however, was having second thoughts about the wisdom of it all. Maybe his boss wasn't so smart after all, maybe he wasn't the best example for a young man, so Louie put the money in a safe-deposit box and found another line of work.

Five years later Rocco was out of prison and ready to take up where he had left off. First he needed to settle his accounts. He called in his gang. Blackie had stayed right where he'd been when Rocco left and continued running the protection racket and high-stake gambling games his boss had set up. Business had grown along with the town. Blackie was now rich himself and returned the five million with considerable interest.

Rocco was exuberant. "Well done, well done. You are the son I never had. From now on you are in charge of everything."

Joey flew in from across the country. He had used the questionable business techniques he'd learned from Rocco and made a small fortune in money-laundering. He, too, returned Rocco's money with interest. Rocco clapped him on the back. "Well done, my boy. I've got a new role for you in the organization. You and I will run the West Coast operations long-distance."

"Now, where is Louie?" Rocco roared. "Find me Louie!"

Louie appeared the next day with the original million still in the envelope Rocco had handed to him five years ago. Rocco was furious. "If you didn't want to use it, why didn't you take it to a bank. You could at least have gotten me some interest?

"The money got me thinking." Louie said. "I knew you were a hard, unforgiving man. You leased substandard houses and then forced people out of their homes when they couldn't pay. You sold protection and then got other people to rough up the suckers who complained. I figured I didn't want to be involved with this kind of money anymore, so I just put it in a safety deposit box.

"You worthless piece of shit," Rocco screamed, and he tossed the envelope with the money to Blackie and Joey. "Take it. It's yours. Now, throw this son-of-a- bitch out on the street," he said weeping and gnashing his teeth.

For those who made it, more shall be given, but from those who have not, even what they have shall be taken away.

Joan King. With apologies to Matthew 25.14-39

NPR AFTERLIFE

When National Public Radio does a series on life after death, you know the question of what happens to us after we die is more than just a religious matter. Religion is personal, but there's another concern, larger than the individual and even more important: What about the human race? Are we approaching some sort of cataclysmic event that will end civilization, as we know it? Should humanity become extinct, will there *be* an afterlife?

Consider the following: nuclear bombs, new and virulent diseases, worldwide pollution, demographic changes that unbalance the social order ... the list is long. Too many educated people are beginning to believe mankind's days may be numbered. I'm not ready to accept that, but I'm sure life as it is being lived in our highly industrialized, corporately controlled society is not sustainable. It's time to get serious about mankind's future.

Most of us believe there is some sort of life after death, but there is no consensus on what that might be. The Judaic scholar Joseph Telushkin believes that "the concept of God is incompatible with the idea that life ends at death." Islam promises Paradise to the faithful, a Paradise where all desires are granted. The Eastern religions lean toward some form of reincarnation.

Along with various theologians, NPR interviewed NYU philosopher Samuel Scheffler. His position is basically non-religious. Imagine, he says, we learn that—without a doubt—everybody on the planet will be gone in the very near future. How would that impact the concept of an afterlife?

Even atheists understand that their own death does not mean the end of their existence. The elements in their body are not destroyed. They turn into something else. The deeds they did in life live on in the memory of others.

In a sense, individual life lives on as long as humanity walks the earth, but what we believe and what we do today has no meaning if tomorrow the earth is devoid of people. Scheffler contends that not only do our descendants depend on what we do today; we depend on our descendants to give our lives meaning.

Contemplating one's own death is difficult enough, but thinking about the fate of the human race is beyond depressing, which is why it's so hard to make people understand extinction is a distinct possibility if we don't learn how to live and work together.

Just as death and the prospect of death don't have to be depressing—I know; I just lost my husband of 59 years—the vulnerability of the human race doesn't have to reduce us to despair. Consider this: Are we an old race nearing its end, or a young race going through adolescence?

Philosophers and theologians alike have suggested both of these similes. I choose the latter. Anyone who has had teenagers knows there is a point when the child slips from parental control: old enough to drive, old enough make his or her own decisions no matter how unwise, and old enough to crash and burn in all sorts of inappropriate ways. I choose to believe our species is adolescent.

There is not a lot a parent can do besides pray. I pray for my teenaged granddaughter and for the human race as a whole, but there are things we can do for our species right now. First we can recognize our own vulnerability. At present, we are trashing our planet. It has to stop.

Next we have to consider the consequences of our acts, not just to our own lives but also to the lives of people around the world. We have to consider not just the welfare of our nation but also the welfare of the community of nations. This perhaps is the hardest of all.

One defends his or her family; one defends the nation. We even defend certain select species,—whales, the spotted owl—but who will defend the human race?

ENDINGS

I have never understood the desire for immortality. To
know that one is mortal, that death is inescapable, is looked
upon as a curse. A worse curse would be knowing you
couldn't die. How awful it would be to know that you must
go on and on with no end in sight! Looked at this way,
death is the ultimate blessing.

Belief in an afterlife is fine, but I am talking about earthly
existence. Here and now, and in the flesh. Here it is, folks:
Human beings are approaching immortality. We're already
replacing body parts, and now we have discovered a way to
rebuild the human heart.

Mankind is creating human life in a petri dish. At the same
time we are endangering living plants and animals all over
the world. If we continue the present destructive trend, one
half of all of the species in earth will be gone within the
next decade. The economic loss alone is horrendous.

Two weeks ago Robert Edwards, now 85, received the
Nobel Prize in medicine for his pioneer work on IVF (in
vitro fertilization). In 1978, when Louise Brown, the first
IVF baby was born, many people spoke out in opposition.
Scientists, they said, were playing God. But today four
million babies have been born using IVF, and infertile
couples around the globe bless Edwards' name.

On the border between Switzerland and France scientists
are delving into the deepest laws of nature to learn how the
material world came into being. The Large Hadron Collider
sends high-energy particles smashing into one another at
incredible speeds in the hope of finding what is sometimes

called the God Particle. If the Higgs boson, its correct name, can be found, it may explain the origin of all matter.

By themselves, these are not bad things, but right now mankind is searching for bigger and more destructive ways to wage war. The U.S. Pentagon wants a new generation of thermo-nuclear bombs. Meanwhile computer viruses are being developed that can disable a nation's security systems. Terrorist cults infect the minds of ignorant people everywhere.

Something is very wrong. We are approaching a threshold of some sort, and there seems little we can do to stop it. One thing is certain; we cannot avoid change. I flinch every time I hear someone say that Americans *must* preserve their life style. It is impossible.

A lot goes through the mind when an individual reaches the end of life. First, denial. Then, anger, regret, and a profound sadness, but there is another almost universal emotion: suddenly life becomes incredibly beautiful. Sunlight on water, the swaying of trees in the wind, a spider web, a raindrop ...are suddenly appreciated as never before.

Perhaps it takes a universal crisis to trigger this emotion in humanity as a whole. Life is precious. Love matters when nothing else does. The world as we know it cannot continue, and scary as it sounds, this is not necessarily a defeat.

Commercialism is consuming our resources. Pollution is making the earth sick. Every technological advancement carries with it unexpected complications. The world is not coming to an end, but something is. It has to. I think we all know it.

First: denial. How many people said climate change wasn't real? Now there's no question. The earth is heating up. Once our economy was threatened with irrational exuberance, now it faces lingering recession. Surely the economy will right itself eventually. Or maybe not.

Next: anger. But anger won't change anything. Take heart. Mankind is one of the most adaptable species on earth, and we have innate inner resources other animals don't possess.

"Love your neighbor." If that's too difficult, just try being civil to one another.

A PERSONAL CHARACTER

We've been hearing a lot about character recently. Opinion columns, letters-to-the-editor, conversations around the water fountain: We want our leaders to be people of character, someone we can look up to.

When I first became a political activist, I believed the solution to our problems lay with our leaders. Elect good men and women. Let them know what we expect, and they will rectify the wrongs of society.

Experience has shifted my viewpoint quite a bit. I have ceased to believe our politicians are the place to go if we want reform, and I distrust a public with an unrealistic view of great leaders who have almost never been paragons of virtue. Start with *The Bible*. King David coveted another man's wife. Faced with exposure, he resorted to deceit, and when that failed he turned to murder. Yet, David was chosen by God to be the leader of his people.

Leadership requires stamina, personal charisma, skill in negotiation, and the kind of wisdom that can only be gained by life experience. Luck helps too. But while we are attracted to individuals who reflect our own values, we need leaders who are equipped to serve the people as a whole, not any particular ideology.

People who run for public office really believe they can change things for the better.

Some actually do, but over time the political system gets corrupted because it is no better than the public that supports it. And politicians, rather than making history, are more often pawns to events beyond their control.

The public, for its part, treats the election of its leaders as if it were a sports event.

"Liberal" or "conservative" are used as rallying cries with very little understanding of the terms or if the terms apply the individual or issue at hand.

Talk show hosts become cheerleaders. Back in 2000 when Al Gore ran for president, a well-known radio personality, in an effort to ridicule Gore, quoted some rambling incoherent answer Gore was supposed to have given to a question about the Mars space probe. The problem is, I heard the exact same quote attributed to Dan Quayle.

Politics have become entertainment, and the public is more interested in confirming its own prejudice and opinion than in hard facts. Facts require research. Opinion requires nothing but a glib tongue.

Politics is the art of the possible, but politicians will offer the impossible if that's what the public wants. There are bills put before the Georgia General Assembly that the sponsors know will not pass Constitutional inspection. Instead of castigating the representatives who introduced them for wasting public funds on costly litigation, their constituents will reelect them for " representing our values."

Election reform is always high on the list of campaign promises, but there is no way any politician can reform a system that depends on money to make it run. Money is the absolute essential in American politics. Until we refuse to elect big spenders, until we develop and support an information system unbeholden to any particular value system, we are fooling ourselves when we talk about democracy.

"AM I MY BROTHER'S KEEPER?"

Everyone recognizes this passage—Genesis 4.9, but what was God's answer? "Yes" or "no?"

God cursed Cain but let him live. People are still debating the outcome: Do we bear a responsibility to our brothers and sisters? Are we not all descendants of the same distant Adam and Eve?

This is what a social contract is all about. We are all connected, but is there a point where the connection is so tenuous that responsibility ceases? This is a moral question, and it usually falls to philosophers and clergy to answer it, so let's turn elsewhere. What does science say?

Science also says we're all connected. What's more, we are connected to everything else in the earth, the beasts of the field and the birds of the air, the creatures that live in the depths of the ocean and those that burrow 'beneath the soil.

Most of us took algebra in school. We know that when something is changed on one side of an equation, something will happen on the other side as well. When one part of our ecosystem is changed, something will happen in response. This alone should explain why we have a responsibility to the earth. Those pesky environmentalists aren't annoying tree huggers. They observe these natural connections and feel a responsibility to act.

Religion. Science. And now ... politics. Let's talk about national health care. Let me remind readers we are the only advanced nation in the world that doesn't have universal health care coverage. We also have the world's highest medical costs. Something is definitely wrong here.

The present administration has passed the Affordable Care Act. Call it Obamacare if you want. It's one more attempt to provide the nation with national health insurance. Supporters know it's not perfect; detractors want to destroy it and start over. Supporters say it's the law; it can be improved but to demolish it is a step backwards. Detractors have dug in their heels and tried over and over again to kill it.

Let's look at Affordable Care from the standpoint of national connectivity. This is how Social Security has worked, and Social Security for all its faults, has been a great help to many people.

Social Security and Universal Health Coverage are part of the social contract a nation negotiates with itself, but it only works when everyone pays into the system. There has to be a single system and a single payer. This is where the trouble starts. Today—and it was probably true to a degree when FDR signed Social Security into law—people don't trust the Government, but who else can we trust with this—an insurance company conglomerate? Wall Street? A single for-profit health czar?

If we care about national security of any kind ... defense, human health, safe food, etc. it's to our advantage to build a system where people do trust their government.

How? By rejecting ideology in favor of compromise, by picking candidates for office who don't make promises they can't fulfill, by refusing to listen to negative campaigns. Some ancient sage once warned the world, "Beware he who would demonize his enemy."

"Yes," I've said, "All governments lie. It's the nature of the beast." We do need to be skeptical, but a rational person can usually tell when a government is lying. This is very different than the kind of distrust we see today, one that says government is inherently bad.

The opposite of government is anarchy. In a time of anarchy there are no guidelines at all. There is no law. There is no social contract. In its place you find the modern survivalist or prepper movement. This isn't just the kind of commonsense preparations we all need to practice. It is a movement based on fear. And fear breeds more fear.

The opposite of fear is trust, not blind trust, but trust in the essential goodness of life.

ABOUT THE AUTHOR

Joan King grew up in New Jersey and moved to Atlanta in 1954 to fly with Delta Airlines. A year later she married Edward Lewis King. Joan and Lewis had three children and a long happy marriage ... almost 60 years.(Lewis died in 2013.)

During their years in Atlanta, Joan studied at the Atlanta College of Art and Georgia State University where she completed a degree in anthropology. In the late 1980s Joan and Lewis moved to North Georgia, where they live on family property in White County. They have one grandchild, Anna Scott King, now a junior at Drew University in New Jersey.

Joan is best known as a guest columnist with the *Gainesville Times*. In addition to writing she is also an award-winning fabric artist and a social activist.

Made in the USA
Charleston, SC
12 June 2016